The Half-Truth High

The Half-Truth High

◆

Breaking the Illusions of the Most Powerful Drug In Life & Business

Kevin J. Fleming, Ph.D.

Foreword by Tom Morris
author of IF ARISTOTLE RAN GENERAL
MOTORS and IF HARRY POTTER RAN
GENERAL ELECTRIC

iUniverse, Inc.
New York Lincoln Shanghai

The Half-Truth High
Breaking the Illusions of the Most Powerful Drug In Life & Business

iUniverse books may be ordered through booksellers or by contacting:

iUniverse
2021 Pine Lake Road, Suite 100
Lincoln, NE 68512
www.iuniverse.com
1-800-Authors (1-800-288-4677)

Because of the dynamic nature of the Internet, any Web addresses or links contained in this book may have changed since publication and may no longer be valid.

The views expressed in this work are solely those of the author and do not necessarily reflect the views of the publisher, and the publisher hereby disclaims any responsibility for them.

ISBN: 978-0-595-45708-3 (pbk)
ISBN: 978-0-595-69641-3 (cloth)
ISBN: 978-0-595-90009-1 (ebk)

Printed in the United States of America

This book is dedicated to the life and memory of the genius we know as CS Lewis.

Thank you for allowing me to find the wisdom to discern the Screwtape in us all

Contents

FOREWORD

"Know thyself!" The advice of the ancient Greek thinkers still echoes down to us through the centuries. And surely, it's important for all of us to know ourselves. It's the foundation for finding our proper path and making our distinctive mark in the world. And of course, it's also crucial in life to understand the other people around us. And we usually can't do that well without first having a good handle on our own behavior. So it's no surprise that psychology sells. Therapists and their books typically promise that elusive bit of self-understanding or that fundamental grasp of other people's behavior that just might make all the difference for us, to change our lives for the better, or at least to help us get along more productively with our neighbors. But how often do they actually deliver what they promise?

Pop psychology has sat atop the nation's bestseller lists since the early days of the old Phil Donahue television show, and possibly even before pop got a microphone. And therapy has long been a part of our culture—at least, in its more urbane and sophisticated circles. When I first arrived at Yale for graduate school in 1974, I noticed right away that nearly all the other students peppered their remarks in lunchtime conversations with phrases like, "My therapist says," or "My therapist is a Jungian and he says"—and then the reply from a fellow student would usually start off featuring a comment like, "Well, my analyst is a Freudian," and then the sentence could almost always have been finished with the confession, "and I'm just as messed up as you are," but it never was—or at least, not so explicitly.

I didn't have to be Sherlock Holmes to spot a tremendous mystery in the halls of the Ivy League, and beyond. The most troubled people I met had usually been in therapy for years, and it apparently had accomplished little, if anything, for them. To make this even more perplexing, some of the least well functioning of these individuals were also advanced academic students of psychology, or psychiatry. They were mastering the concepts and processes that were supposed to be helpful for ridding people of neurosis, and yet they were accomplishing this with apparent immunity to any improvement in their own lives. Finally, to my greatest befuddlement, the most disturbed of the bunch, as far as I could tell, were themselves full time, certified practitioners of these healing professions. And yet, in social settings, they often seemed so chock full of neuroses that you would have thought their patients must have been somehow very contagious. I was quite puzzled by it all. The insights, tips, and techniques for mentally sound and emotionally healthy living that had been developed for the explicit purpose of helping people obviously weren't working either for them or for anybody else.

In this book, the surprisingly normal and emotionally healthy psychologist Kevin Fleming asks why. He suggests that there is something wrong with the typical assumptions that lie behind all the endless therapeutic sessions, and the popular books of advice and counsel by all these therapists and experts, that block their effectiveness. They promise things they can't deliver. And maybe, if we can come to understand why, we can avoid all the endless reading, or the equally incessant talking that all too often goes nowhere, and find some ways to actually transform our lives and our work for the better.

Kevin also sees a parallel problem in the world of executive business consulting and contemporary success coaching. Many magic bullets are sold but few ever seem to hit their intended targets. Why is there such a gap between advice and achievement? With the most advice about success ever available in all of human history, failure seems every bit as common now as at any prior time. Even the publishers who find, edit, print, and sell the best books on business success will ironically admit that they have no idea what it takes to attain a big success in their own industry. How can this be? Don't they read their own books? And if they do, is there something wrong in those books? Or could there be something wrong in how they're used?

Perhaps many readers will find it surprising that the same diagnosis for the most common failures of psychological therapy and contemporary business consulting is also brought, in the third part of this book, into the very personal realm of religious belief. Some believers are saints, and others are just amazing people in whose lives religious perception and discipline have worked wonders. Still others use the tenets of religion in altogether inappropriate ways, to their own detriment and to the great harm of people around them. How, again, does this happen? What's the difference between the promises of religion for a good life in this world, and the results that we too often see?

Kevin focuses his comments in this book on the pervasive problem of half-truths in these three different areas that are at the center of our current cultural conversations, and that impinge on us all—personal psychological counseling, executive business consulting, and religion. His insight is that if we can understand the hold that some central half-truths often have over us in these areas, we can liberate ourselves to shed illusions, embrace the truth we need, live the lives we really want, and perhaps attain the genuine success along the way that we most deeply desire.

What is a half-truth? Well, first of all, it's not a falsehood. There are enough of those around, too, and they clearly cause great trouble to people all the time. But a half-truth can be even more insidious. It is indeed some sort of a truth, but it's often a partial truth that in itself seems to make so much sense that it actually keeps us from seeking the full truth in some area of our lives that matters deeply to us. Because of the incompleteness of this sort of half-truth, acting on it alone can actually make things worse. At its instigation, we end up taking a shortcut, or doing something because it's easy rather than because it's right. Seeing part of the picture gives us a wrong idea of what we need to do, and so we dig ourselves a deeper hole.

Other half-truths can be identified as such not primarily because of their internal incompleteness, but rather because of how they're typically presented to us, and how we accordingly go on to use them in our lives. In this guise, a half-truth can be some sort of general statement about life, or the world, or God, that's complete enough and even fine enough in itself, but that's somehow misunderstood and wrongly applied in our lives because it soothes or feeds an ego need that we have for self-justification or emotional comfort. It then becomes a diversionary path, skewing our focus, and getting us off track for the real insights we need.

By identifying these half-truths in our work and in our lives, we can free ourselves from the problems they often cause us while purporting to bring us solutions. But we can't solve the problems until we can pinpoint their cause. And that's the task of this book. How can this be done? Read on to see how one original professional shrinks it all down to a manageable challenge.

Tom Morris
Morris Institute for Human Values
Wilmington, North Carolina

PROLOGUE

The phone rang at 10:30 p.m. in the winter of 2000 in Laramie, Wyoming, a town full of people still recovering from the savage killing of Mathew Shepherd. Young and gay, Shepherd had been beaten mercilessly by two local thugs who'd left him for dead, tied to a remote fence on a murderously cold night. Many hours had passed before Shepherd was found and brought to a local hospital where he died the next morning. It was in this atmosphere that I found myself the backup on-call clinical psychologist that night in 2000. On the phone was a University of Wyoming campus police officer saying that a young man was sitting on his dorm room windowsill, dangling his feet outside and threatening to jump. We got a lot of calls from drunks or mildly depressed students, but this was serious. Though it wasn't the first time I'd been called out to handle a crisis, this was the real deal—a "live" potential suicide. Driving over to the dorm, I was scared senseless.

As a 27-year-old post-doctoral resident in clinical psychology, I was supposed to know how to act in these circumstances, but I didn't. I'd have to draw upon my own experience and resources, both visible and invisible, as I'd been doing my whole life. I'd have to go past the half-truths psychology had taught me and get beyond the pat strategies of calming someone down. For the first time, I was far outside my comfort zone and removed from the knowledge laid out in textbooks. Now I needed some wisdom and I wasn't sure where to find that. What if I couldn't calm him down? Then what?

When I arrived, I stood out in the hallway and introduced myself, employing a technique called "earning your steps." I just wanted to talk and not come any nearer, until he would let me. Hesitantly at first, he began to speak, saying he was gay and describing how displaced and lonely he felt in Laramie, especially since the Shepherd death. He was terrified of becoming the next victim of homosexual paranoia and violence.

"There are more cows in Wyoming than people," I said, picking up on his isolation. "I can understand your feelings of loneliness."

"I'm all right," he said from the sill. "I'm just fine."

People who are a total mess often tell you this, but his voice indicated he was on the edge of collapse. I didn't think it was necessary to point this out.

"Yeah," I called in through the doorway, "you're absolutely fine."

He said that he'd failed a course this past semester and couldn't go home because his parents would kill him.

Just let me into your room, I whispered to myself. *Just let me in.*

"I understand," I said, keeping the conversation going. Generally speaking, people aren't supposed to jump when they're talking, but this wasn't a general situation. This was a very specific crisis. "What else is going on?" He'd just broken up with a guy he'd been dating and hadn't gotten over this.

"I can't hear you," I said, trying to buy a couple more steps. "Can I come closer?"

After a long pause, he said, "Step inside, but that's all."

I walked over the threshold and into his room.

"You know what it's like to be gay in Wyoming?"

"No," I said, "but with all this going on, I guess it would make sense if you jumped."

He wasn't expecting this.

"Are you telling me to jump?" he said, squirming on the ledge.

"No. I mean your pain is your pain, so maybe all this does make sense."

He was becoming dangerously animated, moving around and crying and going off on his parents. I let him ramble, trying to think of what to do next.

"So you're a therapist?" he said.

I nodded.

"Therapy doesn't help. It doesn't do me any good. I've been talking to all you guys and it doesn't do shit for people. I take Prozac and other drugs and they don't work."

I nodded, feeling more confused than when I'd entered the dorm and weighing my options. Should I try to be super-therapist and start analyzing him from across the room—or try something else? After years of professional training, I was supposed to have the solution, but I didn't have a clue. The only good thing about this was that I knew and admitted to myself that I lacked the answers. If nothing else, I was dealing with reality rather than illusion, even if the reality was overwhelming. Instead of blaming myself for not knowing what to do, I stopped everything for a moment or two and just observed my surroundings.

Looking around his room, I spotted two guitars in the corner, propped against a wall. They were of high quality and in mint condition. For more than a decade, I'd been a musician (mostly a drummer), and music had always opened important doors for me. My hands suddenly itched to get hold of one of these instruments. And frankly, I didn't have a better plan for trying to help the young man.

"You play guitar?" I asked.

"Yeah."

"Then we have a lot in common."

"We do?"

"We both hate therapy and we both play music."

He giggled, the first positive sound he'd made since I'd arrived at his room.

"Mind if we jam a little?" I said.

He looked offended, or at least taken aback. This wasn't how shrinks were supposed to act.

"Ah ... sure," he said.

I didn't make the first move, fearful of breaking the mood.

"Come on over," he said.

I walked across the room and picked up both guitars, gingerly carrying them over to the window. He didn't come down off the sill and I didn't ask him to, but pushed through my own fear and awkwardly joined him out on the ledge. It was uneasy for us to sit side by side in this position, holding the guitars and facing each other, but I was closer to him now in case he tried to jump. In order to fit on the sill, I hung my legs out the window next to his.

"What do you want to play?" I said.

He thought for a few moments. "How about, 'Let it Be'?"

I nodded, figuring I could fake this Beatles' classic enough to strum along. He began to sing in a strong, rich, beautiful voice, putting a lot of emotion into the lyrics—the same depth of feeling he'd just turned on his parents and therapy. His voice captivated me and I followed his lead, harmonizing with him, everything working smoothly between us until he reached the line, "Mother Mary comes to me, speaking words of wisdom, let it be."

He stopped singing, his hands sliding off the neck of the guitar. Sobs poured from him as he shook and leaned back on the ledge, farther and then farther still—toward the open window. I grabbed him by the shoulder and pulled, both of us falling off the sill and back into his room. As we landed on the floor, one of the guitars got nicked, but he was weeping too hard to notice. Catching his breath, he started to apologize.

"I'm so sorry, Doc—"

"Shut the hell up, man," I said, cutting him off. "We just made a CD together."

Both of us burst into laughter, but he was laughing and crying at the same time.

A crisis had been averted and I'd made an unexpected connection with someone in severe emotional pain. Later that night, I drove home with a sense of accomplishment because I'd relied on my instincts, more than my academics, and things had turned out well. Something unusual had happened in that dorm room, something I didn't yet understand. A doorway had opened for me, and the young man and I had walked through it together. Instead of following a prescribed set of behaviors, I'd aligned myself with a deeper impulse than my intelligence, education, will power or other tangible assets, something beyond flowcharts, processes or guidelines.

The next morning I came into work feeling great, my head crowded with visions of being congratulated for saving the young man's life—not bad for my first real intervention. I was in for a shock. Everyone who saw me in the hall before our staff meeting looked away and shunned me. Total silence. At the meeting, the department head started right in, criticizing me for making fun of therapy in front of a potential suicide victim; for playing music and even singing along with someone in a state of crisis; for showing no respect for the boundaries that must be kept in place at all times between doctor and patient. I'd stepped across that professional line and was "too loose" in my actions, appearing more like a psychological renegade then a creative interventionist. In that moment, my professional colleagues felt I'd stopped being one of Us—a professional healer with a reputation and a level of decorum to maintain—and started acting like one of Them—a care-free and impulsive young man. I'd shattered every sacred guideline my boss could think of and he thought of them all. You'd have thought I further damaged the guy rather than getting him back into the room.

"You're still very young, Kevin," he lectured me, "and you're still learning. Now let me tell you what you should have done in those circumstances …"

As I tried to stop listening and feeling what I was feeling, the group began looking for labels to stick on what had happened last night in that dorm room. The kind of shame the young man had felt after coming in off the sill was now filling me up, making me angry and convincing me that something all around me was wrong—at least half wrong. That is, a life focused on how things should have been done, not on how to make them better now. Over-sized egos kill people, I was screaming inside, and psychological righteousness has little to do with being effective in real life. Put more bluntly, "What Freud thinks" is no longer very useful. Human beings could drown while shrinks sat around and discussed the water.

At the end of the school year, the head doctor refused to give me a recommendation. I'd disrupted his sense of procedure—and his profound need to be right. I was stung by his rejection, but today I thank him for his snap judgments of me. Because of people like him, I began to question some of the tenets of modern psychology, and my own involvement with it. This experience motivated and eventually pushed me to reach far beyond conventional therapy and into the broader realms of fostering personal coaching and business success.

At the same time, the beginnings of my illusive half-truth model of life started to rear its ugly head for the first time in my consciousness. The doctor wasn't completely wrong for chastising me. I *was* young and brash, and I had broken some of the rules. I initially denied this and got the empty pleasure of being right, but not happy. Only later did I realize that what bothered me more than his carping was something that lay hidden inside or underneath his words: my job was not to find or even look for innovative therapeutic strategies, but to keep the professional waters calm. The only problem was that the half-truths and psychological formulas the instructors were using didn't go far into the process or mystery of finding real solutions or optimal responses to human conflict or pain. I was grateful for my training but I wanted something more than worn-out reactions and half-answers.

A half-truth is always a representation of some part or aspect of a situation. But if we take it to be the whole truth about that situation, we can go dangerously wrong. I've come to feel that psychology is full of half-truths. So many popular books and feel-good gurus trade on half-truths. We are always in danger of falling for a half-truth if it gives us enough to validate our first reactions to a situation, eases our discomfort, and keeps us from doing the hard work of penetrating through to the full truth of the problem or problems we confront.

If a man's death was prevented on that defining day for me, yet it led to nothing but criticism, what incomplete truth was in play? Why was this obviously good outcome overridden by the need to prove me wrong? How many times in the "normal" flow of business and life were we operating on this same half-satisfying and compromised level? What was it costing us in terms of suffering or wasted dollars and cents? Did the field of psychology get lost in method over meaning? These questions shaped and drove all my future work.

I didn't save that student on the ledge because I had all the answers. I didn't just get lucky either. Even though I truly didn't have all the answers or solutions to his problems, what I discovered was that my having all the answers for him isn't the sort of "full truth" we should be looking for. Instead, I discovered what was present at the moment that allowed the two of us to bring him safely off the ledge. What we did together in extreme circumstances—and co-created—I do every day now in the world of private counseling and business consulting. I work with patients, employees, and executives to move past the half-truths and inappropriate conceptions of what counts as the full truth, and then to discover with them the opportunities they couldn't see before. This book is fundamentally for people who don't merely want to be comforted, or put at ease, or have their previous views reconfirmed, but who constantly strive for that elusive *more* yet end up with less in what seems to defy logic.

About 80 % of my clients are in that population where information doesn't change them. Telling, prodding, pointing out, pushing, convincing, and outlining a plan doesn't cut it—no matter how "right" the ideas are. There are now 5,421 book titles on Amazon.com that have the "Seven Secrets" in their title. It's hard to see how there could actually be as many as seven secrets about anything at this point in history with so many such books out there purporting to reveal what has long been hidden.

But as a professional shrink of a distinctive sort, I have a take on all this. In an effort to shrink the best of the best of success secrets down, this book turns over the top secrets to see what is much more crucial to understand if your goal is actually change—the half truth that lies silently on the other side of these cleverly trumpeted and ballyhooed quick tips. Ever try to bargain with one of those seven secrets or tips you read about? To see how you can maybe keep one foot firmly planted on one side of the fence still doing something you don't really want to change about yourself, while seeming to follow the quick tip fix? If you have, then you've been bitten by a pseudo-attempt at transforming your life and this book is for you. It uncovers the always present and insidious **half-truth**—the REAL key of change to confront head on—that eludes the best of the best success-oriented books because it sits underneath mere information or advice, like a germ spreading and outwitting the best antibiotics.

Why are people today so enamored of these so-called "reality TV shows?" Because the number of us living in illusions has grown to vast proportions; we want to escape into the pseudo-reality of television and watch people whose problems are actually like our own, but seem so extreme that it gives us reasons to deny this and merely fall into an entertaining, mind-numbing zone. This is a wonderful half-truth system that keeps honest self-reflection at bay and statements like "Can you believe that poor idiot?" spewing from our mouths and distancing us from both the characters on TV—and ourselves. If we actually lived in reality, in a fully conscious way, there would be very little appealing about running cameras 24/7 on what is really our own dysfunctional behavior. We wouldn't feel so smug watching these shows but would silently and authentically connect with that seed of similar pain living within all of us.

In my research, I've found that good habits form not just by practice, but by unlearning the illusionary aspect of our behavior hidden beneath each well-intentioned tool that's offered up to us for fixing that behavior. In every truth offered up for positive transformation, there is a half-truth lurking and enticing one to believe that by living the half-truth you are "basically" or "for the most part" doing what needs to be done. If you have a success book on your shelf, and its potential is gathering dust, maybe you need a model of ***unlearning***, of behavior change, not just a clever new piece of information. A book on un-learning your "should do's" first in order to learn a new "would do." And the result of that is not just coping or lowering your confusion. It's bringing together the discipline of psychology and the engaging spirit to find wisdom.

In the psychological industry, many therapists and authors have become immensely successful selling half-truths and, let's face it, for some people that works well enough. Or at least, it appears to. But I don't know if these methods really heal or transform anyone, or ever help anyone to find optimal responses or real solutions to their problems.

If you're tired of just getting by and want to get beyond that, if you've applied every infomercial program to yourself and still feel something's missing, seen enough therapists to last you a lifetime, or are merely curious about whether your definition of success can weather your self-undermining tendencies, welcome to the future—a future of more of what "really is."

RE-THINKING SHRINKING: THE SIX HALF-TRUTHS of PSYCHOLOGY

So much of the discipline of psychology is about reducing "cognitive dissonance—" a fancy way of saying "reducing stress." This kind of reduction has its place in therapy and can be useful, but I often find myself asking a different set of questions: What's on the other side of the dissonance, if therapist and patient can manage to push through it, instead of just trying to lower stress or rationalize their own roles? What happens if you confront the dissonance head-on, rather than tip-toeing around it as if it were your enemy and should not be provoked? What if it's not your adversary, or work to be processed through unwillingly in therapy, but your actual ally, your very best ally, and its job is to get you to pay attention to the stress so it can teach you something? What if our core job is to discover what's it's trying to teaching us, and then to implement that lesson? What if that "lesson" is there to "lessen" your pain the next time the same conflict arises? What if instead of *just* getting less stress, you also get a life that's not only significantly more open to change and creativity but:

Freer
Evolving
More Real
Complex but not complicated

And you get to uncover parts of yourself you never knew existed—parts that are there to get you past just coping and onto the next level, which is about transforming the pain into something new and useful. Then you can do great things for the sake of doing great things: the essence of a life well lived.

Many will disagree with me and say, "Traditional therapy helps people and tons of folks can attest to this." For those in crisis, this is arguably true, but for those who aren't—and those with more complex and nuanced goals—"help" often resembles the effects of anesthesia, a numbing of the pain to avoid "getting real."

The real value of busting through dissonance versus relieving it as therapeutically necessary goes far beyond "self discovery." We usually have enough "self" to last us forever. What I'm talking about actually transforms the world—by losing the self more. Not in some impossible super-Zen sort of way, but in a way that allows even those with narcissistic personalities to choose better results over their "need to be right." Who wouldn't pick health over sickness or recovery rather than just being right about your diagnosis, while remaining ill?

Not long ago, I had the distinct honor of being invited to hear John Mroz, President & CEO of the globally influential East West Institute. His organization has been innovative in engaging warring factions around the world and helping them find peaceful solutions to their problems. In essence what makes this institute's interventions better then traditional government-to-government "first track" dialogues is their ability to build trust for discreet conversations between the parties. From the tearing down of the Berlin Wall to positive outcomes with China, the East West Institute has mastered the art of engagement, believing that the more one disagrees, the more engagement needs to happen. Because they can leave egos and agendas at the door, and walk through it with the utmost anonymity, they've had world-class results. The East West Institute is a wonderful metaphor for what psychologists <u>could</u> do if they gave up their "pathology dialogues" with patients. These embody the traditional conflict resolution approaches of "healing" someone's flawed position for a win-win outcome, instead of going to a deeper level that could transform not only the patient, but the therapist as well. In the spirit of transformation, I want to identify the following six half-truths that keep psychology locked into old patterns and predictable results.

Half Truth #1: Emotional processing is the core of therapy.

We were told in graduate school that the way to lead a patient to his or her goals is through the path of emotional connectedness and verbal expression of the deepest kind. As a therapist, this meant looking or listening for something that would knock your socks off: the patient articulating with feeling words or strong visual evidence of "being moved." Or, on the other hand, looking for a patient who showed the opposite of these things. This equaled "resistance," which was just more grist for more therapy of the same kind. Either way, it was great pretzel logic and could easily be a dead end. Just because someone was expressing strong emotions didn't mean the feelings were authentic; and just because I was helping this person get the emotions out didn't mean we were accomplishing anything. It was all about playing the game, rather than winning it. Once the game had been defined, it became a thing unto itself.

How could I measure the authenticity of the responses I brought out in my patients? Nothing is more elusive than feelings; they flip-flop from one to the next from moment to moment, and all can be real or un-real in that instant—not the best validity system out there. If we utilized the same system for making distinctions about whether or not the foundation of a bridge was stable, we'd have lots of cars in the water. If I could be convinced that genuine emotions were overwhelmingly present, I was trained to reinforce continually such a flow of expression as if it were needed for change. In this trap, a psychologist can easily believe he's fully engaged with the healing process and yet go on autopilot. All he has to do is keep the "continue-to-emote" needle injected into the veins of the person who's letting it all out. If we don't like the person who's being expressive or articulate, we've washed our hands of that responsibility and can label him a "charming narcissistic sociopath."

Shrinks love labels. When I was in graduate school, I dressed up as Elvis Presley one Halloween and stormed into a multivariate statistics class playing my guitar and singing, "You Ain't Nothin' but a Data Point!" I jumped up on the table and had the instructor dancing with me as we sang my lyrics, which did a pretty good job of rhyming words like "Bonferroni" and "Non-Parametric-"—a result worthy of the King. Observing the room for whether this stunt was rather foolish or quite engaging, I opted for the latter as my lanky, tweed-laden, bearded professor busted some moves for the class while shining a smile the size of Texas.

However, in my review that semester, the faculty said I was poor at "self monitoring" and had "low self awareness." The next semester I toned everything down in order to make a better impression on the staff. They said I was "withdrawn emotionally" and appeared to have lost that "joie de vivre" that made me who I was, provoking dialogues with me about an insecure and compliant identity. What did any of that have to do with my reality as I was living it and trying to find some humor and enjoyment? Where was their authentic effort and interest to understand who I might actually be? Or were they only concerned with passively reflecting the behavior of their students into some easy label that matched their DSM-IV world? They seemed much more comfortable with half-truths and knee-jerk reactions than I ever was.

They had to protect and maintain their own professional world, which took great pride in reductive thinking about the emotions or needs or desires of the individual self. At the time, it made me wonder: Could psychology truly handle studying the difference between eccentricity and pathology? Friend and colleague Dr. David Weeks, a neuropsychologist at the Royal Edinburgh Hospital in Scotland, felt the same way I did and embarked on a powerfully insightful qualitative investigation of these two constructs that took him around the world interviewing people who may not have been "normal" by our best social definitions, but seemed to defy standard psychometric analyses of pathology. While they embodied the eccentric personality, they not only didn't fit the crazy persona, but actually revealed some unique benefits compared to most of the "normal' people out there: better immune systems, hardier and more resilient personalities, extremely witty senses of humor, and robust sex lives. Perhaps in my grad school years I was attempting to carve out a place for this misunderstood population, and was a bit ahead of my time. Perhaps the reason my grad department couldn't quite label me was that I was onto something outside their well-defined categories, something worth attending to—worth listening to, and I wanted to pass on this wisdom to my eventual clients, later on in therapy. But that was to be quite a challenge too.

As I went into practice for myself, what struck me was how accessible the autopilot button was when conducting therapy. I could doubt falsely, or believe for the wrong reasons, the character, motivations, and intentions of my patients and still be hailed as the facilitator of a great session—and get a check and another appointment out of people. Where was my alignment to myself, to them, and ultimately to truth and reality?

I believe this quagmire arises from the difficulty of building a scientific method on "input data" that are both suspect and vacillating—those ever-changing human emotions. They are very few actual basic emotions and we as a society have created others (i.e., feeling "bad"), which really are mutated combinations of other feelings. To be in this emotional processing realm in the truest sense is to be a linguistic policeman, disentangling What Is from What It Feels Like, and this can become exhausting and nearly impossible. So we simply ride the emotion train instead, nodding at everything that comes out of a patient's mouth. Emotions are BOTH the most real and most illusory guidepost to a richly lived life. If we are to build a field on such a powerful tenet, we have a moral responsibility to know emotions truly—not just label and note them.

All this really hit home for me the day I tested my emotional intelligence with my boss in a start up company where I was Director of Training and Development. In an effort to help us understand the EQ (or Emotional Quotient, as it's now called) of our hires, we found one of the most objective EQ tests out there (the MSCEIT) and used ourselves as the supposed benchmarks for what constitutes high EQ before we administered it to others. What we found was that we had horrible EQs. And what was the response of my boss—also a psychologist?

"Lets not use it," he told me. "The test must be faulty."

We had a choice to make—to be open and flexible to unearthing a potential threat to a strongly held personal belief system, which for my boss meant shaking up more than 20 years of telling himself a comforting story about how emotionally healthy he was. He wanted to take the path of least resistance and scrap the EQ tool—a quintessential example of cognitive dissonance reductions at their best—or worst. I chose instead to take in the test results and think about them, using them as a "maybe" in my life that needed to be listened to. And to this day, I still think the test was right.

What do I mean?

First, what psychologists infer to be emotionally intelligent behavior day to day with patients in psychotherapy can be done in quite an aloof and, ironically, emotionally disengaged manner. The methodology is not *necessarily* a mirror to how Daniel Goleman, a leading guru on emotional intelligence, actually defines the full, comprehensive idea of being an emotionally intelligent human being. His definition discusses

4 relevant areas of functioning that go into this construct of living with a high EQ. They are:

1. Accurately perceiving emotions in one's self and in other

2. Using emotions to facilitate thinking

3. Understanding emotional meanings

4. Managing emotions

Though these 4 areas would certainly sound like the natural elements of a standard psychologist's session, there are elusive half-truths to each one of these definitions, starting with the accuracy notion in Number 1, that can insulate a therapist and keep him/her from penetrating into the realm of authenticity with a client. What do I mean?

How "accurate" am I in the perceiving the emotions of my patients? Can we ever really be sure since we have the power to diagnose a disorder of thinking and brain chemistry? Sure, patients will clarify our attempts to understand them, but at the end of the day, most of my patients would not give up the needle in the vein that they receive in unconditional positive regard *as a whole* to quibble over the accuracy of a perception of an emotion on my part. I believe this is a value trade off that people make unconsciously or consciously. And at the end of the day, it really isn't about the accuracy of the reality in and around us—it is about feeding the system of feeling good about the reality in and around us, something that we'd be hard pressed to give up. And once accuracy is compromised in a process so amazingly strong as the practice of psychotherapy, the rest of the components of EQ, in my opinion, get further entangled in the illusions of being half-right. Domino effect 101.

So therapists easily fall into the elusive trap of feeling emotionally intelligent when we're really just intellectually astute at articulating—from a distance—the *language of* emotion and emotional connection. On that day when I stared at my own test score, I had a choice either to look at it honestly or deny its meaning. I was instantly flooded with memories of how I used to be that high EQ kid and how graduate school had slowly displaced my ability to be emotionally intelligent with the prideful intellectualizations and rationalizations that won me friends, respect, and noteworthy academic accolades. This was hard for me to face, but a necessary truth: I'd won a Ph.D. but in many ways had lost the rough and more interesting and empathetic edges of who I was.

In learning how to succeed in the professional world of psychological certification, I'd started to ignore how to connect and to help others have their own transformational experiences, while ironically carrying the "certified psychologist and expert on emotion" card. I was becoming more "normal" inside my own shrink-wrapped subculture and less helpful outside of it.

Some people become theologians to keep the real demands of spirituality at arm's length. They are masters of the language but are strangers to the realities involved. Physics offers another parallel. The language of physics and really knowing physics are two very different things. You can teach a clever parrot some of the lingo of physics, but that doesn't make him a scientist. A scholar who can memorize theorems, articles, and knows the "facts" of physics is also not thereby a true scientist who can leap into any problem dynamically and find a solution. A real physicist can use the language and categories of the science, and he can invent new language to discover the true reality of a problem. Then he can also teach it or explain it to others—in different ways to different people who are in different stages of readiness or intellect—and reveal the miracles of the physical world.

The same is true of that form of emotional understanding known as empathy. When becoming a therapist, I was trained in a system of empathy that had nothing to do with my heart. My words were rated on a scale of 1-5 from basic to advanced empathy, as my instructors needed some way to measure me objectively. But I wasn't allowed to talk about the possibility that the level 5 professional therapist and the level 1 patient could have something important in common—which is that both of their internal dialogues might be saying, "Get me the hell out of here!"

We were always told to bring our full authentic selves to the therapeutic role, but in many evaluative contexts throughout my education in the profession this always resulted in some form of disapproval. Though we were taught in theory to strive for the opening up of a real dialogue with patients—the key being to transform the world and its pain through listening with the mind *and* the heart—something seemed missing between what we were supposed to do and what we were rewarded for doing. Because we were taught to settle for so much less, we were destined to follow robotically the half-truth that convinced us we were right—the often empty or threadbare claim that emotional processing is at the heart of therapy.

Half Truth #2: Our job is to reduce pain and suffering.

We've had a hundred years of therapy and the world is getting worse. I love this concept, which was put forward by James Hillman. How could this be, if we so doggedly have worked to reduce the pain and symptoms of many generations? Perhaps we've sought an extreme understanding of the weaknesses and pathologies of human beings, not knowing that to connect with them and influence and change them, you can't know just the dark parts but must know all the other parts, as well. What if change comes not from fixing the bad parts but from realigning the interplay between how the "*good*" and "*bad*" (or as I prefer, the "*real*" and the "*illusory*") have a dialogue and the resultant meaning they create? Can you have a true understanding of an exceptional piece of music, such as a symphony, without taking into account the moments that are largely absent of sound?

In our quest to help other people and maybe, in a way, to seek our own "perfection," we frequently define that help as "reducing their pain." How can we not be doing a good job if we take a self-reported depression severity rating of seven and drop it to two on some questionnaire we have purported to be an estimate of "truth of depression"?

What if reducing the pain is exactly the opposite of what's needed spiritually in order for true accountability to be learned? What if love (in many ways a nasty four-letter word in psychotherapy) is really what's needed and, further, is best understood as honoring the natural process of things? By this, I mean that perhaps a real therapy guided by love is a sort of process involved with sowing and reaping, a Newtonian every-action-producing-an-equal-and-opposite-reaction kind of thing. What if therapy-as-we-do-it-now is actually messing with that? What if "I'm okay, you're okay," is nothing but a half-truth disguised to make people feel good when what they really need is something else? What if this lack of judgment about us doesn't mean that we're actually being appropriate or even virtuous in our decision-making? And what if it's not okay to repeat the same foolish mistakes again and again?

Let me put the cards on the table. I believe that God wants us to learn from our missteps, not just to do them over and over, while feeling better about it all. And God wants us to create new things, which is why this inherently feels so good when we do it with our selves or others. Even if you leave God out of this, wouldn't you still want this outcome for yourself?

If you keep repeating your mistakes, and you don't have a therapist working hard to convince you that you're just fine andyou can learn to feel fine about it all, the pain will get worse. That is the only way many people can learn. So what's the point of briefly alleviating suffering if it assists us in reinforcing our most disruptive and destructive habits and patterns? For therapists, it's another dilemma that many try to duck. The larger question for us becomes, "Should we just plug up loopholes in the psyche or should we look for sustainable solutions?" I think we should search for the latter. And I'm in the company of some cutting edge thinkers, like Henry Cloud and John Townsend, whose books on boundaries have been incredibly successful.

All of this is why "loving our patients" has been so taboo and seen as a dangerous slippery slope (wrongly equated to erotic encounters between patient and therapist). Bringing "love" into the session work—the kind of love I'm describing here—would bring with it the hard lessons it teaches and could cause a conflict between accountability and unconditional positive regard. Not to mention the other problem of its conflict with our long-term habit of focusing only on symptom reduction. One can have far fewer symptoms and still be quite unhealthy: push on the bubble and the displaced air pressure will make it pop up somewhere else.

Most arguments against a full paradigm shift would say, "But some people need symptom reduction and others need transformation." That's true, but therapy isn't a fast food drive through, and I don't take orders or deliver only combo deals. Do we all really know what we need for our own growth … or do we know the best shortcut to the appearance of getting the growth we say we desire? The client-centered approach appeals to the hedging part of us: how can I have one foot on this side of the fence with the old paradigm of seeking just to reduce suffering temporarily in a "whatever it takes" way, and one over there speaking the language of authentic change and real therapy?

Getting past the half-truth of feel-good psychology—that our main goal is helping people to just feel better—will alone allow us to get both our feet on the side of real growth. This half-truth is a half-truth precisely because feeling good is a good thing, but only if it results from a better reality, and getting to that reality is what really demands our attention, rather than just the feelings.

Half Truth #3: Our job is to increase happiness among humanity.

"Another thing that is troubling to me about [promoting] a positive psychology is that it can foster a tendency to ignore or minimize attention to what people are actually experiencing in the world. It suggests that we can fix the world by fixing the way people think about it. What is troubling … is that often, people are miserable for very good reasons. And if we were able actually to develop a positive psychology of hope, then perhaps we would know how to make people happy without very good reasons. I would rather see us finding a way to make people happy for good reasons, but that would suggest an emphasis on … finding ways to change the world rather than changing the way people think about it … My concern about changing cognitions rather than changing the world can be summarized as follows: when the world needs changing, we should change the world and not how people think about it."

"Pitfalls on the Road to a Positive Psychology of Hope," by Barry Schwartz

This brilliant perspective underlines the dangers of postmodern thinking that have recently riddled our profession. Like the swinging pendulum, we must be cautious about getting too caught up in either traditional psychotherapy with its focus and near fixation on pathologies or in the "positive psychology" movement that's now gaining so much attention. In my graduate statistics classes, I learned that the tail ends of the bell curve are where disorders and mental illnesses lie, while the 68% of the population in the middle is roughly called "normal." As I listened to a confident recitation of these numbers in my psychology class one day, something didn't seem right.

This split on the graph between normal and pathological would eventually become the basis for the booming positive psychology field, but it struck me as another enticing half-truth. Who could argue against the goodness of studying hope, joy, and humor, as opposed to hallucinations, delusions, and abandonment traumas? Maybe it was the Elvis-singing part of me that always looked for a reformulation of the accepted, but I found myself taking issue with this bell curve premise and the way it was being used. I wanted the class to consider that a subtle but dangerous assumption might rear its ugly head down the road:

If pathology were really believed to occur only outside the majority population of "normal" people, the positive psychology movement could easily "accentuate the positive" and just deny the hidden pathologies in all of us, including the 68% of us in the normal middle. This wouldn't lead to more happiness, just to more self-righteousness and less accountability. For me, another psychology class ended in disappointment and I felt as if I were screaming in a vacuum with insights that seemed more like out-sights. No wonder I hit the bars and played music for money every night. By about midnight, the whole bell curve would start to flatten out quite nicely.

We *can* thank positive psychology for coming along and saying, "There is more then just pain reduction necessary for living an optimal life." And I agree: virtues of increasing hope and joy are essential to the good life and we do need to know more about how "normal" minds work. But what if we don't really need much more of an understanding of the "normal human being"—or to keep reinforcing the language that marginalizes "pathological people"—as much as we need to seek and create a new synthesized and integrated model for all of us. "Normal" and "pathological" are not mutually exclusive realms. There are a lot of pathologies operating inside of normal people, and the separation between the two groups is never that clear-cut. You need black in order to understand white, just as you need white to grasp black.

All professional psychological notions of "Our model is more complete than yours" miss the essential point. We're not living in an either/or world but a both/and universe. I understand that the positive psychology folks claim that prior psychological models have concentrated at the tail ends of the bell curve, so we need an understanding of the 68% who fall under the bulk of the bell curve. But that 68% also needs to be willing to examine the illusory aspects of their "normal" lives and be open to looking into those secret places where their own pathologies can be found.

The positive psych platform says that we need more exploration of normal people, but I'm saying something quite different: normal people aren't really so normal, after all. Or perhaps, better: normality doesn't equal health. We simply need to look at the bulk of the bell curve with fewer labels and a more discerning eye. It's time to move away from this normal versus pathology mentality and toward an overarching mindset that distinguishes what is real versus what is illusory—*even without the presence of actual clinical delusions or hallucinations, and no matter where one falls along the bell curve.* It's almost enough to make you think that the attempt at defining pathology so strongly and definitively by clinical standards actually increases the crazy and unreal levels in us all (i.e., "At least I am not THAT crazy …"). By contrast with clinical pathologies, we can allow our own problems to remain and even grow and think we're fine. Maybe an integrative shift needs to happen. When you make this shift, you bring together the whole curve AND find the place in all of us (schizophrenic and healthy) for directly confronting pathology and engendering hope. So the half-truth that our job is just to study the happiness to be found among normal people and then use what we learn there to simply increase the overall happiness in humanity generally misses the truth. That truth is that we all need to understand the realities of our lives, in their positive and negative aspects, and work toward greater strength in how we function. Happiness is nice. Who wouldn't want it? But there are more important underlying realities that need to be addressed if that happiness we seek is ever to be real and lasting and right.

Half Truth #4: My Reality, your Reality—it's all good.

In many ways, the traditional practice of psychology brings up an odd contradiction: we're postmodern in our acceptance of you, but if you do something really weird or if enough people complain about you, we'll label you crazy. We teach not to judge another's experience and we're to accept his or her reality, but then we are prepared to use therapy stories when we feel we need to, in order to build the case that something's wrong with you. If anyone doesn't believe this, sit in the lunchroom of a counseling center or group practice and hear what is really said about other human beings. It's as if we don't truly know what acceptance is or means—to therapists, it often means accepting someone's take on reality until it goes outside the realm of some vague line of what we think is real. Said another way, acceptance ultimately ends up being a Catch-22 for the patient. They may "do what it takes" to get that warm fuzzy feeling from the shrink, but it could, in the end, be what ultimately hurts them and hinders them from being able to generate solutions needing more than just affability and validation.

We have all heard the saying, "Love the sinner, hate the sin." If not, it means that we must be active in drawing the line between the action or behavior and the person as a whole. This makes sense, right? Though it has a very natural appeal to the intuitive part of us all, to actually follow through with the call for this distinction would also inherently mean that there is a clear courageous part of us all that does JUDGE a behavior (vs. being judgmental about a person). By virtue of this distinction, then, how could a relativist position be taken on people's actions? Doesn't therapeutic validation potentially anesthetize this critical, discerning life force in us all? I argue it does, even if we misuse it in a benevolently intended way.

For this principle to be appropriately applied in the practice of psychotherapy, we'd have to employ it fully and honestly, and I simply do not believe that's what we do. In potentially refusing to challenge rather than validate, we cheapen our language (our currency of accountability), and we end up using and throwing around snippets of wisdom (i.e, love the sinner, hate the sin), while disregarding contexts, purposes, reality, etc. This is similar to how fundamentalists take quotes out of the Bible and use them as weapons. Politicians are also well known for doing the same with isolated statistics and poll results. If we truly believed this tenet in the practice of psychotherapy, we'd have a lot less tolerance for the illusions created by our own category schemes, and we would be more rigorous in how we describe patients and the subtle but important differences between them. Simple labels would be replaced by critical thinking. We'd also be less tolerant of the illusions our patients often cling to, while excusing them as their "realities." We'd be more willing to call people on their use of trite phrases designed to make them feel good, rather than to be applied effectively in our day to day lives.

In my practice, one of the most common examples I've seen of this "Let's have it both ways" kind of thinking is this: people talk of the need to forgive a person who's done wrong by saying, "Sure I can forgive, but I can't forget."

Many therapists and patients see these two concepts of forgiving and forgetting as completely independent and nearly irrelevant to each other. But are they really? If one practices true forgiveness, it doesn't erase a memory but *transforms* it—not in factual content but in what the event will be taken to signify and how it will affect our perception of that person now and in the future. It also creates a new understanding of the usefulness of the event for teaching us what we need to learn. If we can truly forgive, and grasp what forgiveness means, then this eliminates the need to make a case for an act of forgiving without altogether forgetting. And then there is no need to spell out the difference between these two words, either to ourselves or to someone who might have offended us. This gets to the source of the memory problem, instead of just treating the symptoms. And then we can truly go forward and leave the past where it belongs—behind us—while taking its positive and helpful lessons with us.

The good intentions behind the half-truth of "my reality, your reality" may be based on the often-beneficial consequences of being non-judgmental, but sometimes we go too far in that direction and fail to take a stand that needs to be taken. Not by choosing my reality over yours, but by choosing the encompassing reality that serves all of us better.

Half Truth #5: Accountability is crucial.

In psychotherapy, we've created this half-truth to mean: we hold our patients accountable to appointment times, action plans, payment schedules, and what they said in the last session. But is this TRUE accountability to its fullest? Does it mean that if they aren't late for their sessions, we've done our jobs? Or are we celebrating mini-successes as we undermine potentially larger wins in areas that really matter?

I sometimes think psychologists discuss accountability only in those arenas where their own power and control can be most clearly manifested. We like having authority over others and being able to exercise it. In much the same way that we love ourselves loving another (instead of simply loving the *other person*), and we love talking about how we talk about psychological constructs. Intellectually processing or discussing emotions versus truly living in a high EQ state are two very different things. Talking about accountability and really embodying it are, as well.

One of the best examples of the accountability dilemmas for shrinks is a section of the American Psychological Association Ethics Code related to patient-doctor sexual relations. Though it clearly prohibits this act during the course of therapy, it states (or implies loudly) that sexual relations with a former patient after two years of terminating the professional relationship MAY be ok but the burden is on you to prove that it wasn't exploitative:

10.08 Sexual Intimacies With Former Therapy Clients/Patients

(a) Psychologists do not engage in sexual intimacies with former clients/patients for at least two years after cessation or termination of therapy.

(b) Psychologists do not engage in sexual intimacies with former clients/patients even after a two-year interval except in the most unusual circumstances. Psychologists who engage in such activity after the two years following cessation or termination of therapy and of having no sexual contact with the former client/patient bear the burden of demonstrating that there has been no exploitation, in light of all relevant factors, including (1) the amount of time that has passed since therapy terminated; (2) the nature, duration, and intensity of the therapy; (3) the circumstances of termination; (4) the client's/patient's personal history; (5) the client's/patient's current mental status; (6) the likelihood of adverse impact on the client/patient; and (7) any statements or actions made by the therapist during the course of therapy suggesting or inviting the possibility of a post-termination sexual or romantic relationship with the client/patient. (See also Standard 3.05, Multiple Relationships.)

What is fascinating about this is that a section b) is needed for those not getting the message in a), and is still lax in terms of accountability. Two years? What is magical about this number? And how could a relationship post-therapy not, by definition, be exploitative based on the strategic techniques of empathic connections, implied one-way soul wrenching stories, and the exchange of money? Despite these concerns, it would seem that the APA is comfortable showing that they've taken charge of protecting clients and building a profession based on accountability.

There are two important concepts here, really, and they can be represented by something as small as upper and lower case letters: Accountable (Big "A") and accountable (little "a"). And there lies the "half-truth" rub. Perhaps "little 'a'" accountability is really about: Did we follow the rules outlined and can we make a good case to support our rule-based decisions? And "Big A" accountability is more about transcending the rules—however good they might be—to move to a place where scorecards don't matter, the place where the heart and the internal dialogue of one's soul kick in. And there, rules or no rules, we do the right thing just because it is right.

There are many things that may not be wrong but are also not fully right. If you doubt this and don't have any stories to back up my claim, take a lawyer out for a drink and get him to speak to you honestly. I know, you're probably saying to yourself, "Easier said than done." But take my word for it—it's worth the effort. Of course, some may read this and take offense, which is not my intention. And I don't have the lawyers in mind here but the psychologists who may think I'm being unfair. For there are indeed those of us who try to be accountable in the deepest sense in the work we do.

For example, some psychologists take pride in honest self-disclosure about the negative things that patients and doctors sometimes do in therapy ("I'm sorry, I just nodded off a bit ... I'm late today because ... I'm so sorry if what I said came across as too harsh ..."). The shrinks are quick to call themselves or patients out on these minor problems, believing it's all about holding people accountable. But I don't know many who will call themselves out on more subtle yet brutally honest kinds of things.

One time, after listening to a patient's story, I said: "Wow, that was very interesting, John. The way you were able to see how your wife—wait, no, I take that back. There was nothing interesting about it, actually. I sometimes find myself mechanically saying something when I really don't mean it. Do you ever do that?"

Before you all send me hate mail about my lack of empathy for my patients, I ask you to take a breath and listen to the most bristling section of that feedback to this patient. Was it really that I said to them that their story was not interesting? Or was it more in the *invitation for us all* to get uncomfortable and challenge all our automatic patterns that keep us mechanical in our exchanges and, ironically, less authentic—despite the words we use to indicate otherwise. Could a richer dialogue emerge from this piece of feedback then a mere rote response of something being "interesting." I believe it does, as the heart and its inner voice will always be more of a compass of truth than many of the words we use in actual conversations. But don't take my word for it. Take it from yourself and your memory about the countless times you wished you really knew what someone was thinking about you while you were talking to them.

Despite my rougher edge on the surface, this piece of feedback was at least an effort at accountability with a capital "A," first on my own part, catching my use of a catch phrase when I could have been speaking more helpfully and, in the situation, catching my patient pinning something on his wife when he should have been holding himself more accountable for his own behavior. This is a very different application of accountability in the therapeutic context, instead of just blaming someone for being five minutes late. To me, true accountability means checking one's automatic responses in situations even when nothing NEGATIVE has happened. It's making a habit of not allowing oneself to become mentally or emotionally lazy.

As I suggested earlier, when things feel good, make sense, and you are nonetheless wrong, it's because you've only half-asked and half-answered a question. So you've only been half-accountable to your profession, your patient, and yourself. When I say that the belief that accountability is crucial is a half-truth in psychology, I mean that the concept is too often used in as cheap and easy a way as possible and not with the proper depth and application that makes it a real and genuine truth.

Half-Truth #6: Psychologists are healers.

Are we? This is a fascinating topic for many reasons:

1. I think that sometimes we heal and sometimes we don't and, therefore, are not true healers, vocationally speaking (yet we could be).

2. I think we still don't have an operational definition of what healing is.

3. I think we equate healing with alternative forms of medicine, thereby implying, in the dominant traditional medical model, a lack of healing.

4. I think there's a big difference between care-taking and care, and the latter is the stuff of healing, which can happen only when we take the time and make the effort to truly care.

5. I think that, if we wanted to be healers, we would have to get rid of the fear that riddles the profession. This kind of fear is not of the knee-shaking kind but is manifested in critical distance and self-protective, right/wrong orientations. It's a higher class or more evolved type of fear, so to speak. But it's still fear. And it's a real problem.

6. I think that true healing can't occur in a session that doesn't talk about love, God, and the transcendence of linear thinking, causal models, and mechanistic actions.

7. I think that we can reduce pain and do nothing to heal another human being. And we can increase happiness through a positive psychology movement and still do nothing to really heal anyone. What if we can be ultimately happy with our unhappiness at times, somewhat like the martyrs and saints

were on the way to death? What if, to get to this place, we need to heal our afflictions within by killing our illusions and unhealthy bargaining strategies and by living coura-geously—living, not just to be happy, but to be real.

I feel that psychologists should not live to give advice—usually quick, pat advice—but to help patients uncover their own reality and genuinely live that. Yes, I can hear you shrinks now who are reading this thinking to yourselves, "Duh, Kevin, that is what we do!" To which I would say—not wanting to be too complexly polemical: "Really?" For the whole process of therapy is about what the therapist thinks, whether that is expressed in a long prescriptive dialogue about what the patient should do or in a disapproving glance of the eye or, most elusively, with a clearly critical, elongated silent pause from the psychoanalyst. In essence, to heal as a psychologist, we must teach peo-ple to fish instead of giving them a fish. Or perhaps it should be said like this: We need to teach people a "virtual reality game" of how to fish.

When a caller phones Dr. Laura and she scolds and then fixes him in one minute and he thanks her profusely for her efforts, she's handed him a fish. If he called me, I'd try to show him a principle of reality that would lead to a response like this: "Wait, I think I've got it. I can not only change my marriage with this, but it makes me think about my relationships with my friends, my children, my boss, and all those things I said as a kid to my mom." I'd hope to teach him to fish by concentrating on something other than "fixing" just one problem. And, in this understanding, one sees that fixing is not healing. Care taking is not care. This is not to say that we're not ever helpful at all in the standard transactional work we do but that, many times, we're not true healers.

All of this has been written following the April 2007 incident in which a 23-year-old Virginia Tech student, Cho Seung-Hui, murdered 32 people on campus before killing himself. After this event, the field of psychology took a big hit. Practitioners were cited for not identifying Cho's potential for doing harm or for not doing more to prevent this tragedy. As I watched the post-massacre coverage while preparing for a call from a national TV news organization that had asked me to comment, I thought about many of the things that form the basis of this book.

It is a universal, existential tendency to deny our vulnerability—one more way of trying to lower cognitive dissonance. We typically think we are immune to "extraordinary" 9-11 type pain, while accepting the regular difficulties of everyday life and maybe the prospects of a lesser accident or even a bout with cancer. But our brains fail to wrap around the notion that normal, unfortunate pain and 9-11-level pain have in a sense EQUAL probabilities—if not literally, then at least in the "anything's possible" sense in the grand scheme of life. We have a tendency to deny the possibility of extraordinary pain and to keep betting on "low pain" options, but that does nothing to stop the killer hand from being dealt. The tendency is there to make us feel better and encourages us not to confront the source of or potential for violence within all of us.

Psychologists are severely ill-equipped to deal with this kind of mass tragedy in the aftermath of which shrinks come on TV and bellow about the "shoulds," while putting themselves forward as "experts." The themes they love to talk about are "prevention" and "warning signs." This is NOT what I'm writing about. I'd like to see a major paradigm shift that, though it may not prevent these things in the future, will assist us in grounding universities and other institutions—any organization of group of individuals, in fact—in a more reality-based acceptance of things that we often choose to deny. Colleges and universities need to understand that:

1. College student counseling centers need more innovative, dynamic psychologists who are more than just label lovers or safe, antiseptic professionals and who, as a result, can change lives.

2. Outreach programs with dorms are outdated—college students need more hands-on coaching and engagement.

3. Treating the symptomatic pain of students doesn't cut it. Trying something different, while it may not prevent a future disaster, statistically speaking, may transform the students IN GENERAL. Isn't that a more "positive" outcome to strive for than just hoping to do things to reduce the likelihood of pain?

Perhaps we should be filling the TV studios with experts on healing, not experts on illusionary feel-good dialogues concerning all the 'what ifs" that are intriguing to hear but that really do nothing for our capacity to heal. We actually build up an immune system to prevent healing when listening to the more clever rationalizations from experts about what should have been done.

The half-truth that psychologists are healers falls short because of what we too often are, not because of what we truly could be. We may sometimes serve to heal feelings now, but we could heal much more deeply if we broke away from what is so easy and, instead, did what is right.

INSULTING CONSULTING WITH THE SIX HALF-TRUTHS of BUSINESS

As I prepared the content for this section, it hit me that I will upset many business self-help writers and consumers out there. Oh, well. Both the people writing those books and the people reading them are often content in their complacent worlds of easy affirmations and simplified to-do lists. I'm here to say: "It's more complex than that." But the way through that complexity is to first identify and become aware of the half-truths underneath some of the most common success myths out there.

In this section, I name the common "Business Success Factor" that can be found in the mouth of nearly every supervisor known to mankind—they're just too tasty, too good, to argue about. And for many there is a kernel of truth inside each one. I then unpack them and show the half-truth lurking in there: the illusion that actually keeps you from the success you were supposed to get by following that Business Success Factor in the first place!

Put down your *Wall Street Journal* or that latest highly effective success tip book and prepare yourself for what is …

Business Success Factor #1: Don't Sit Around Wondering About What To Do—Just Do It!

Half-Truth #1: Search for most of the elements in your life where the "Just Do It" attitude has gotten the job done and use that as your proof that you are getting done things in other realms of your life where in reality "just doing it" misses the boat and all of the complexity, nuances, and under-the-radar screen issues that are REALLY needing address by you.

We live in a time when action rules. The thinker on the rock in the most notable of pensive poses has become quaint—a symbol perhaps of the leisure to just think or ponder or, worse, of rationalization, denial, excuses or passivity. The guy hunched over with his chin on his hand clearly isn't getting much done. Nowadays, in the corporate world of eat 'em up and spit 'em out, there is unbridled passion for the zest of growth, wealth, or just "progress"—anything that keeps us "moving," always moving toward a goal. Let's look into this concept a bit further.

Movement doesn't always equal improvement or evolution. As an African proverb says, "Don't push a river," meaning: we sometimes have to let things move without the need for friction or effort. Many of the instances in my own life that arose out of the advice to "Just do it" ended up being the causes for problems and pain. But how could that be? I had initiative, drive, passion and the supposed intelligence to weather any storm. Such is the burden of being bitten by a half-truth: it always makes sense. For a personality type like mine, taking a risk was practically innate. And when you regularly act just to take risks, you usually "win" just the right amount of times to convince yourself to commit the same "sin" again. That is the power of intermittent reinforcement—one of the greatest psychological truths of our day and the founding template, proudly enough, of such different phenomena as the Stockholm Syndrome and those heaps of cash lost by millions every day in Las Vegas. Win-win-win over and over, strangely enough, is not the strongest way to get addicted to something. You're actually more reinforced to keep rolling the dice by a pattern of win-win-lose-lose-win-win-win-lose, as you become wrapped up in the power of unreliable inference and hopeful anticipation. You can interpret a partial correlation as a probable causality and come to mistake happy accident as destiny. Such is the power of half-truths.

Through intermittent reinforcement, we seek to preserve our secret sense of a God-like status and declare, "This is the way it is," when, in reality, we remain perceptively flawed and shortsighted human beings. From my understanding and application of neuropsychology, both in my work and my personal life, I've had insights into business, relationships, and, yes, even God.

First, we're all motivated more by reducing dissonance than by increasing consonance. Despite what we might consciously think and say, we're more moved to avoid pain than to achieve gain. The brain is wired more by reinforcing the instant of relief it experiences when some tension gets minimized. As in the gambling example of Vegas, one win can eliminate the accumulated tension of three or four or even more losses and completely convince you that you ARE lucky and should continue. It doesn't say to the mind, "You had a chance moment of luck and it could break any time, so now is a good time to walk away."

As a psychologist, I've seen countless examples of this among my patients who are having extramarital affairs. Very rarely at the beginning of an affair do they get a cue that they should simply walk away before more damage is done. Too many other cues are saying, "Keep going," or, "Since there are no immediate negative ramifications, there's nothing telling me not to keep going," so they do.

Secondly, the brain cannot literally multitask. It is literally and theoretically impossible. Though we divide inputs into the information-processing pipeline into nanosecond differentials, this still remains true. This leads to a huge implication for teaching and learning: we may appear to simultaneously learn as we are doing, but learning with true efficacy and accuracy is a practiced ability, not innate like the mere infinite processing speed of the human brain. Said another way, practice makes perfect, no matter what you're doing.

Simply "doing" without focus or concentration is another half-solution to problems. Science is just beginning to provide evidence for what this really means. In his brilliant article, "Theory of Sequentially Timed Learning," James F. Cassily wrote, "Our ability to *correctly* learn is a learned ability.... To discover why some genetically normal brains are able to learn more efficiently than others, we need only ask the deceptively simple correct question: 'What single learning related attribute do the world's greatest scientists, athletes, CEOs, artists, astronauts, philosophers, mathematicians, musicians, etc., all have in common?' One must logically conclude that such highly successful individuals tend to have excellent focus, the ability to selectively concentrate for extended periods of time without interruption."

In the West, Cassily argues, the mental ability known as concentration is largely something that science and psychology believe we are born with, so there hasn't been much effort to understand what it is or how to teach it. But it's much more than innate skill. "Our rapidly expanding understanding of the human brain," he wrote, "is helping us to recognize that many of our children's most detrimental cognitive, motor and emotional problems are simply the result of *bad habits*; and thus are not written in stone. To the contrary, the more fundamental these acquired habits are, the easier and faster they often are to correct. Early diagnosis and corrective intervention can quickly bring about dramatic changes in a child's learning abilities, self-image and conduct; and their productivity and overall quality of life as adults.

"Less than 1/10 of one percent of all humans are currently performing at their peak genetic potential level of concentration. The rarity of *professionals* who are able to consistently excel in sciences, arts, sports, music and other lucrative high skill related careers is indicative of this estimate. All children deserve the opportunity to reach their full cognitive, physical and emotional potential. Early diagnosis and corrective intervention are absolutely critical to providing them with a more equal opportunity to do so."

In his acclaimed book *Flow, The Psychology of Optimal Experience*, Mihaly Csikszentmihalyi wrote, "People who learn to control inner experience will be able to determine the quality of their lives, which is as close as any of us can come to being happy. Although in its present state the human mind cannot do what some people would wish it to do, the mind has enormous untapped potential that we desperately need to learn how to use."

So instead of saying, "Just do!" to every task or challenge, I prefer to say, "Just master." Action is important, but action without concentrated mastery can be counter-productive. And that's why the common focus on action alone provides one of those half-truths that we need to understand, so we can avoid the problems it otherwise leads to.

Success Factor #2: Have a Vision of the Endpoint In Mind.

Half-Truth #2: It's important in any pursuit to, as soon as possible, define a vision, set goals, follow through, and use initial feedback from that beginning process as proof you are on track. This not only reinforces any mental associations that may have been weak to start with, but it can also keep you from hearing or seeing evidence that your choices aren't working.

Does my identification of this as a half-truth mean I think that, in any situation where positive accomplishment is a possibility, one should just sit back and do nothing? Quite the opposite. Recognizing the common recommendation of quick goal setting as a half-truth propels us to look into "appreciative inquiry" and to be open to all the stimuli we encounter. It also persuades us to listen even more closely to the counter-evidence in front of us, especially when we are comfortable with our apparent success, feedback, rewards, and general place in life.

That, of course, is easier said than done. Setting quick goals around a mere endpoint, despite its "clarity," is not what's important (for there is a fine line between clarity of vision of something and clarity of reality). Setting the right goals is. And then continuing the spirit of inquiry that helped in the initial goal setting, as the process continues, is just as important. If we are open, we can learn things along the way that any fixation on a quickly set, or even intelligently set, goal can prevent.

We live in a constant neurological battle of cost/benefit ratios, with ongoing trade offs that we want to ignore. It's not that we don't understand all this—it makes complete sense, as does most of the advice your mother gave you as a kid. But now it's more about being willing to give up something that "makes sense" in order to explore another choice that can lead beyond "making sense" and into "wise action." Who really wants to do that? It can feel like giving up 100 dollars for 50 dollars. Or like the law of "necessary and sufficient" that we learned in algebra class about mathematical properties: certain things are necessary but not sufficient. It makes sense to start any enterprise with goals. But just having vision goals isn't sufficient for success. We need wise goals. And we need a wise process of seeking to attain those goals. While it might make sense to "begin with the endpoint in view," satisfying the mere criterion of "making sense" is often not enough—not when it leaves out other qualities, like virtue, ethics, and complex decision-making. These are all built on examining and employing higher conditions of logic, sustainability, replication, and universality, and they require a different mindset.

Much of the popular success literature and, for that matter, most of psychotherapy and consulting alike, is in love with the initial analysis phase of change: figure out what is wrong and tell someone that. Pointing out the inconsistencies in a system, a life, or a process can be like describing the flames that are burning down your house. An insight is a form of helping, but there are many false celebrations about this. The "aha" we get from clients in business coaching sessions after laying out a strategy issue they executed poorly, especially when the "aha" falls into the "makes sense" category, does little to transform anything in the coaching session or in the person looking for help. It only temporarily makes the client feel better about what's going on and merely on the basis of what they just said. Coach and client can then fall into the illusory trap together by falling in love with what makes sense, not with what makes change really happen.

It's the oldest pattern in any of the consulting/helping professions. The person needing help, or change, sets out by defining a vision and a goal, while the helper monitors that path, calling each step progress and taking payment for "the journey of self development." How can anyone go wrong? Everybody wins! (Wait for more on *that* half-truth later on).

Such is the insulated bubble of consulting, which can easily reinforce the very notion it promises to undo by trading the overdone-with rationalizations of a company's "here's what's wrong with us" list for the more empirical sounding rationalizations of an "expert." Without a lot of discipline and commitment to getting beyond just "making sense," the process can merge self-as-observer and self-as-God into a potentially dangerous time bomb. None of us has a God's eye view of exactly what goals we need to set and how we need to pursue them without a lot of hard work and hard thought, and this won't be instantaneous or quick. To encourage and praise goal setting and pursuit *per se* as if it is always good, regardless of how it's done, is certainly a dubious enterprise. And all the while, the whole process may be creating more disconfirming evidence that any of this is actually working. Yet that, too, is often ignored by the person needing the real help: "Well, she/he IS the expert who's been hired, they must know what they're doing...."

Taking a bullet out of a brain as a neurosurgeon is a bit more deserving of the deferential reaction "He is the expert" than the case of a consultant taking thoughts, feelings, and concepts out of a mind. If the premises for our expert statements are made from external dialogues and not the internal dialogues where change or resistance to change truly comes from in those we work with, we are risking diluting the wisdom of the expert construct. For the neurosurgeon, an MRI confirms accuracy. In many helping professions and consulting practices, it's far harder to determine any form of accuracy. Ask corporate directors of training if they ever subject their external consultants, trainers, and coaches to any sort of ROI test and have them follow up on actual hard-core behavior changes, let alone financial changes inside the business, after a training seminar. As with patients who just accept mediocre therapy, this lets the "experts" off the hook.

So what are we to do about this hyper goal setting advice and the insistent need for vision found everywhere in success books? Are they all wrong? No, they hold just the correct amount of right to confuse you. And that's the classic nature of a half-truth, isn't it?

Has anyone ever explored the occasional benefit of having no vision and setting no goals and written about that? If anyone has, it certainly hasn't hit the best-seller list recently. I would argue that, in certain contexts and at certain times, this is EXACTLY what the doctor ordered. Why? What if through intermittent reinforcement you've been unwisely convinced that your vision is right and even have some recent "proof" to show you are right? This is often true for the gambler in Vegas suffering from the delusion of over-confidence. It's also often true for the manager or executive who sees a lack of overt resistance from his employees, along with perhaps a blip of positive news that may or may not have anything to do, causally, with that vision, and yet concludes from all this that his vision is, indeed, right.

So am I saying have no vision at all? Well, no—not literally. But you often have to take your time to create a proper one and then work hard to have one that is malleable, moveable, testable, and breakable. Have one that can adapt to the ever-changing conditions of business and of the human beings who make business work. Don't think you're God, and don't think you're Moses—none of it should be set in stone. And for those who hold so tightly to their vision, having none for a while may be the best de-tox tool of all. To say that we all need a vision and a goal is a half-truth precisely because what we need is a good vision and wise goal and a proper process of enacting both. Otherwise, we're often worse off than having none at all.

Success Factor #3: Make Your Pile of Priorities.

Half-Truth #3: Get jazzed that, because you've graphed your urgency and importance matrix, you've adequately addressed time management effectively, while ignoring that many of your perceptions for each factor actually come from reactive parts of your brain (thereby violating Success Factor #1).

Making Priorities? How can any advice related to this be even remotely indicative of a half-truth? I'm not saying that this skill isn't helpful. What I am saying is that an explicit process like this is more helpful for the person who otherwise normally completely fails at building priorities into his life than it is for someone with more natural ability in this area. In many ways, what I'm getting at can be found in the "opponent process" model of addiction. There are two motivating cycles in addiction. First, the addict takes the drug to "increase the positive feeling" that is created by the substance. Then, unbeknownst to the user, the motivation switches from that to "decreasing the pain of not having it."

So the success tip we read everywhere about making priority A, then B, then C has unique benefits depending greatly on its context. For some, the probability increase for success happens more because of the setting of priorities (i.e., those who really are struggling with even getting started). But for others, success is not enhanced by merely writing down priorities, which has become part of the business vocabulary of achievement. Many follow through with this exercise simply because, if they don't, they feel they're not true students and practitioners of success. It's this population I'm mostly talking to now.

For the man living on the extreme end of the bell curve of orderliness—in a state of chaos—it's quite beneficial to make priorities and get one's head straightened out. Any such intervention will likely help this person. But as you move towards the middle of the bell curve, toward the "average" person, the accompanying motivation may start to switch away from a benefit-oriented perspective towards a deficit-oriented perspective. Do top-of-the-bell curve people really need to have better priorities or are they dealing more with the challenges of bringing their goals to completion? They may be "making priorities" in order to hold off or deny the far more complex and uncomfortable feelings of an emerging "mid-life crisis" or other forms of personal unhappiness. Explicit exercises of priority setting may function in the lives of some people as one personal version of whistling while Rome burns. They may need to explore the underlying reality of their situation far more than making a list for plowing ahead. In fact, it's this that they should prioritize.

One of the best ways to confuse the human race is to take any good principle and then substitute for it a simple, simplistic slogan or buzz word. People nowadays often throw around words like:

Success
Priorities
Goals
Vision
Maximization
Productivity
The American Dream

Then they mix them all up, as if a virtuous life is simply a blend of these ingredients tossed together in 1) any order and 2) any amount. A chef would kill you if you told him that his most delectable dish could be made in any amount and any order. Why do we ever buy into the wisdom of avoiding this like a plague when it comes to food, but have far more difficulty doing so when it applies to living itself or success? We are inundated by half-baked slogans that may go down easily, but watch out later! Why do we ever fall for this in life when we don't for a moment in the kitchen?

The answer is sensory reinforcement and sensory correction. We get immediate feedback in the kitchen from our taste buds that something is right or not quite right or very, very wrong. There is no "seventh sense" (assuming the sixth is intuition) of a "success taste bud" that turns its back on the overindulgent or under-cooked success recipe. In fact, we eat it up more readily because it sometimes briefly satisfies us, as fast food does, without being good for us. It gives us a false sense that we have the handle on what it takes for success without any of the hard work it really takes. Like any half-truth, a recommendation of the benefits of prioritization can blossom into a full truth and path to real success only when we do what we need to do, beneath the level of activity it suggests as sufficient.

Success Factor #4: Smart Negotiations of a "Big Picture" Type (win/win)

Half-Truth #4: Because conflict can be unsettling or worse, it's crucial to reinforce in yourself the belief that any given solution you propose truly is a win/win and not just a weak rationalization that everyone benefits, even though someone actually does "lose" in some sense.

This one gets at the conflict between commitment and compliance in human nature. Once we've been bitten by the "win/win" half-truth, we quickly seek agreement, or even just appearances of agreement, no matter what the sticky internal dialogue unfolding within us might be concerning what is being ignored or compromised. In our rush to create a harmonious looking solution, we often can miss opportunities to examine a deeper commitment to a more fulfilling or longer term plan. All this inherently violates any law of sustainability. The only way an action is sustainable is if the underlying value orientation is aligned toward that *at all costs.*

The words used in a committed dialogue and the words used in a compliant dialogue may look the same. As in many of these half-truths, the deeper truth is not always obvious to the human eye or ear. But if we stand for nothing in our negotiations, then we can fall for anything. If we don't examine the core values underneath the words and don't take a genuinely values-oriented stand, we risk forsaking truth for lack of conflict. And we know in philosophy that the presence of a positive is different from the absence of a negative.

The corporate training world is really affected by this half-truth. If there's not a visible or glaringly evident problem, this gets equated to "Everything is fine" or fine enough not to disrupt the system that's in place and apparently working. Some researchers have started digging below the surface to learn more about what executives and employees really mean when they talk about business conditions.

Richard Barrett and his National Values Centre have developed a method of consciousness assessment that can help a consultant decipher or distinguish between two otherwise "equal sentences." For instance, a Level 2 consciousness person who has "skills with people" is quite different from a Level 6 individual with higher order engagement and connectedness capacity, yet in a taped interview they may sound exactly the same. The exact words can have very different meanings depending on the context. The cultural transformation tools put out by Barrett's team of consultants, of which I am one, help convey to clients where the best investment lies in uncovering dormant values that can be highly powerful in decision making.

Win/win scenarios may always look good in some way, but they also can get a serious "push back" from reality. Let's face it, if you try to make a good deal with a bad person, is everything fine as long as each party gets what they want? Is the appearance of harmony in the deal enough to create a genuinely good situation, long term? Or doesn't our world sometimes require win-lose scenarios? If Darwin had been fixated with a concept of the ever-harmonious win-win in everything, he'd never have uncovered natural selection. Win-win can't always prevail in an often win-lose world. And we can't let the quest for surface harmony prevent us from examining the values that must be preserved and then insisting on their preservation, come what may.

Now for the first time in this half-truth model, we see the connectedness and cumulative effect of each half-truth as it relates to the others. In the language of integral philosopher Ken Wilber, this model is "transcendent but inclusive." What do I mean? Each principle is tempered by the others and should be consistent and aligned with all. We have an acknowledgment of an often win/lose world, but if we don't see the loss in its fullness and grace, we risk perpetuating another quest to win inside of a losing battle.

Analyzing your "loss" does not equate to "Seeing the silver lining in the otherwise dark cloud." That is yet again another feel-good drug that superficially gives you the sense of evolving in your way of thinking. Finding a momentary "cup is half-full" insight does NOTHING to truly align you to life unless you believe this: "In every loss, there may be peaks of hidden goodness and truths, but even in that I remain still vulnerable to missing the completeness of the meaning of this otherwise unfortunate event."

That is wisdom. And it is wisdom that is not taught by even the most astute psychologically-minded business consultant who simply reframes events from one incompletion of dissonance into another incompletion with consonance. I'm seeking something else, something more elegant and inherently complex: a sometimes-dissonant, sometimes-consonant completion.

Success Factor #5: Get a deep, 360°, self-detached understanding of the other's position.

Half-Truth #5: It's important to seek to understand but to do so as a technique and hope that the other party won't see that you're using empathy so strategically that you've become inauthentic.

After more than ten years of business consulting, psychological training, thousands of coaching sessions with clients, multiple CE courses, seminars, workshops, discussions with colleagues, and endless readings, writings, and onsite observations in and on emotional intelligence, I'm convinced that this remains one of the most abhorrently unexamined half-truths out there in business. Put in a nutshell: talking about emotions and being aligned or connected with another human being may be close in terms of words but worlds apart in the ramifications on that other human being. In much the same way that Cloud and Townsend have written about boundary violations that seem full of love but are actually full of hate when one disguises the latter in the former, it can indeed be a diluted version of hatred. Or at least an act of controlling another's right to choose freely.

I speak from direct experience and carry this 'sin' within me. I've had a hard time forgiving myself for the countless business coaching sessions where I took money and received praise but was not really present. Why? I did everything I was taught to do when interacting with a client, yet I was leaving out "me." It was the spiritual rape of both the consultant and client. The business field is full of training courses that don't take this deep level of connection into account.

Is this thing called "presence" important and can we use it in ways that go beyond hiring an engaging speaker or an inspired-sounding leader? Yes. And can we train for this quality? The answer is also "Yes, I believe that we can."

If we could truly focus on removing the things that we think we need and were willing to confront what is often uncomfortable in our thoughts and feelings, we would naturally spend more time with "What Is" and less time in the seductive world of illusion. We'd become more present in all circumstances and this could become an ingrained good habit, as opposed to the bad habits of avoiding discomfort and not being present when that's the easy way out. This kind of concentration would then be automatic and effortless.

So much of empathy training is about two linguistic elements (a statement and a response) that are designed to lower conflict and seek consonance—instead of working *through* the dissonance and getting somewhere new. The client says X, Y, Z and we are supposed to unite X, Y, Z, into a summary statement that's comprehensive and gets at the primary emotional experience around the event. Nothing in this process is about discovering "What Is" but about aligning our words into an optimal understanding of their world of perceptions and feelings. Is empathy just an untruth wrapped most stylistically to adjust one's own comfort level to another's emotions?

I was taught to match and reflect back to another human being his or her view of the world—not the world itself. I was not only ultimately doing that person a disservice but myself a disservice as well. Inauthenticity bred more inauthenticity until I no longer knew the true and virtuous things of life. And if I didn't know them or couldn't recognize them, what chance did I have of really helping that person?

I once wrote a song about this called "If I Were To Love." It came to me after attending a retreat and realizing that my extensive and successful psychological training had actually contributed to my own illusions about love. In loving myself for loving others, especially those whom I narcissistically dubbed as my "social projects" in need of my divinely inspired help (NOT!), I became so insulated that I couldn't experience the actual giving of true love—the kind that forgets the self and leaves its indulgent, manipulative parts in the dust.

Any insistence on the strategic importance of an appearance of understanding is a dangerous half-truth. The real truth will always involve genuine empathy for its own sake. And only that can truly have good results.

Success Factor #6: Brainstorm Non-defensively Creative Solutions.

Half-Truth #6: It's important to brainstorm beyond reactive first gut solutions to convince yourself that you are co-creating an "optimal solution."

I believe one should not only pause once before being tempted to make a quick judgment about a person or event but actually pause twice, instead. Why?

The first pause is necessary just because we often use the too-smart part of us to hesitate for a moment for the *appearance* of not being blatant about attacking someone else. So we tell ourselves we are successful in a negatively phrased sense—that is, we did NOT hit someone or verbally respond in the most extremely reactive manner so, therefore, we have become non-reactive. However, during that pause, we often just plan and refine our coming attack in a more covert way, thus rendering the first pause utterly useless, ultimately, if our goal is not just "to avoid inflicting overt pain on someone else" but to then DO the right thing. We have traded not hitting someone or withholding an instant verbal lashing for a prideful intellectualization of the event that will eventually erode us in a similarly blow-to-the-head kind of way. If we can get past this pause and then pause again, we are on the more evolutionary road to truth. But this second pause is so hard for us, and it tends to be completely ignored by anger management theorists who are still working on the first pause all the time! And imagine a team of 10 around a table having to exponentially learn this same lesson noted above. Quite the challenge indeed but worth "naming it" upfront, rather than assuming that mere brainstorming and the head nods that result do away with its difficulty.

Most of business negotiation training, psychological consulting, etc. is based on the "First Pause" and is presented as an airtight case of employing both restraint and wisdom. The internal dialogue is: "Okay, you want to hit this guy but don't do it. Really think about it. Do you want to that bad? Is it truly worth it? Take a deep breath and let that mammalian brain not react and you'll be fine."

This is merely a symptom-relief type of approach that leads to another misperception:

"Symptom reduction—> decreasing reactivity—> optimal responding"

But nowhere in this chain of psychological thinking is there a filter for what constitutes an optimal response. We get only the "lack of a reactive response."

The point here and the point of this book is that most of our success barometers stop right there, without a search for what is optimal. To go any further means exploring yet another round of discomfort, and that is what I'm asking for.

What we need is an understanding that discomfort is often the precursor to break-through truth and that it should not be reduced. Most virtuous decisions in mankind, individually and with groups, were made right after allowing and examining this type of feeling and thinking. Brainstorming is a helpful process, but its good qualities come more from listing and grouping activities that are of low risk precisely because we pre-condition people to know that "There are no wrong answers."

That may be true ... for a little while. And yes, I understand that brainstorming is often a necessary step in the right direction of creating innovative solutions. But it can be used as an illusion for the manager to appear as if he "put issues out there to be explored" and can be used to let employees hide their own internal dialogue and conflict. The implicit assumption underneath brainstorming is that "everything is possible." If systems theory has taught us anything, it's that this simply isn't true when it comes to a homeostatic system of optimal output for all the wheels turning and reinforcing an aspect of business culture that teaches that that is not beneficial.

Like the children's t-ball leagues that now give everyone trophies because he or she showed up and participated, "Everything is possible" may be good in the beginning when building self-esteem or just for getting ideas and combinations of ideas out into the open. Yet it has to be understood as potentially beneficial within only the strict constraints of a very limited activity or set of activities and for a specific purpose. We shouldn't build it up or preserve it as any other part of the world of fully functioning adults living in a complex system of unintended consequences of our actions.

When I began integrating deeper understandings from these six half-truths and communicated them to those I worked with in my consulting practice, my consulting sessions changed dramatically for my business clients—and for me. In one company, our work together increased productivity by over 50%, not by the use of any MBA-endorsed consultant model but through an unexpected intervention: I coached the leadership team on changing their conversations. How did that happen?

The team had convinced itself that improved productivity would come from "getting to the point" faster, by cutting the length of their meetings in half. Result: their actions actually *decreased* productivity! They were clearly bitten by the half-truth of "making priorities" and "being smart with time and not having unnecessary meetings." Doesn't this make sense? Half-truths always do. But shortening their meetings put increased pressure on everyone to play the game a certain way, and they felt an overwhelming obligation to get more done in a hurry: "Who cares if we're committed to a useful result.... We're done, aren't we? And faster, too!"

I showed them that it wasn't the time frame that needed to change but how they spoke to each other. For a month, we went back to the traditional length of the meetings but threw away agendas, Power-Points, protocols, and to-do lists. I instructed them to talk to one another with no expectations of what to say or how they should interact. "*Just be co-creative*" was the advice, which was highly unnerving for these Type A, hard charging personalities. They struggled initially, but soon found an increased sense of communication and authenticity. More got said and more got done. It wasn't time itself that mattered but how they perceived what was truly important in every moment. Their meetings had been dominated by false assumptions, which led to useless results. By fixing or eliminating those assumptions, they might as well have gained the ability to create time itself!

In the above model, easy ideas of good and bad lose their meaning. The sacred half-truths that we too often worship fall to the side and *everything* is potentially useful. The results flow from an approach that the executive development field calls the "360 Evaluation." Although this tool has been around for a while, it's often turned into a subtle Us vs. Them model of ranking a candidate in a pass-fail sort of way. In my work with corporate managers who think their company's culture is broken, I move them beyond the notion of where they think they **should** be to what they **would** do in various value-conflicted scenarios that elude the most rigorous of 360 tests. In other words, we co-create entirely new possibilities together by choosing to not be satisfied or complacent with "a successful score." Beneath every high percentile rank is a buried half-truth feeding the executives wonderful rationalizations for why they were ranked so high.

Recently, an executive in Boston wrote, "Dr. Fleming initiated the formal 360 Evaluation; facilitated the survey analysis and reports; and, conducted a thorough feedback session with me. Having had some experience with other profile-assessment tools ... I thought I knew what to expect. I was wrong. The reports and accompanying information were, quite frankly, superior to anything that I'd ever imagined. Reviewing the results was like seeing an x-ray of my life. I was able to quickly and clearly see how I was essentially coping with life—not setting myself up to thrive. Accompanying the 360 results was a three-ring binder, explaining the various indices and findings. I learned how people really saw me every day. My peers, my bosses, my friends all registered their constructive opinions on my behaviors and actions. There it was, in black and white: how I ranked against the best leadership qualities.

"I shifted my view that I needed to rise to a job opportunity, to realizing that I secretly wanted a new job to give me self-esteem. I switched from thinking that I needed to leave my 'bad self' behind, to understanding how important it was to actually embrace my vulnerable characteristics. And, for the first time in my life, I saw a pattern of apologizing for my uniqueness, instead of leveraging it....

"Accompanying this report, was an action plan encompassing ... a values assessment, maintaining a blog of my evidence of 'the myth of invincibility' in all areas of my life, and developing a clear model of change, highlighting the pros of 'staying the same' vs. the cons of changing (the man I want to be)."

And from another executive in San Diego, "The number of destructive dialogs I have had with Tim have dropped by 75% or more. Both Tim and Rich respond almost instantly to the needs for my area of work, so they no longer inadvertently block my progress on tasks. Also, regarding interactions with others, I am studying my dynamics with each individual and noticing how slightly changing my approach to requests and things is making large differences in the response I get both in the willingness to do the requested work and the attitude toward both me and the work requested by me."

Both of these execs first had to know what their reality IS before any change could take place. In each case, I had to hold back and not "do" anything "to them" until they'd had this realization, which is antithetical to every other training or consulting model out there. In other words, I had to hold back on the "just do it" half-truth.

Many CEOs are at a loss as to why teams don't perform, their business culture is not accountable, and they feel betrayed by fellow executives, or at least not truly and completely aligned. The common denominator in example after example is the conflict between accountability and fear. CEOs unconsciously build teams around themselves that in the short term will respond to a false sense of bravado, security, and the *need to be right*. That one need always erodes enthusiasm, breeds passivity, and robs a corporate culture of verve and creativity—the lifeblood CEOs crave in their people. While leaders wrongly conclude that their staff is incompetent, the staffs conclude that their leaders are out of touch and *unrealistic*. Robert Hurley has noted in *The Harvard Business Review* that 69% of 450 executives from 30 worldwide companies agreed with the statement, "I just don't know whom I can really trust anymore." Perhaps there can be no trust in half-truths and partial successes. Perhaps trust needs full-truth in order to breathe.

Isn't this just another way of admitting that our own front-line thinking is badly flawed and out of touch with reality? To change this, I ask my clients to consider six fundamental questions before beginning the "360 Evaluation" itself. The questions go deeper than the normal two-dimensional data typical of a feedback session:

1. What is the half-truth that keeps me believing that this present reality is good enough?

2. Can I embrace the present moment critically yet non-judgmentally before acting out any new game plan?

3. Am I merely reducing fear, or am I increasing creativity by embarking on this new choice?

4. How much of my certainty to move on something is emotion (or basically reactivity), and how much is wisdom (the appropriate mingling of emotion and reason)?

5. Do I want to be right or *do I want to be truthful*?

6. Am I willing and ready to go all-or-nothing on following this path and willing to stop bargaining?

If you own at least one self-help book with the number "Seven" and the word "Secrets" in the title, you can see that these questions elude the quick tip model out there and are essential to understand before making sustainable change. The stakes are higher than ever and clarity of intention is critical in ambiguous business situations measured in nanoseconds.

Applying these questions, while uncovering multiple half-truths, unleashed a net gain of $4 million in a venture capital situation. It would have gone unrealized *simply because of false assumptions and a single false inference* on the part of a principal in the primary investment firm—a bright professional "in touch with" standard success practices but unaware of what was really controlling him. In other examples, a health care executive with a great idea found the way to help decision makers who formed a coalition of providers, all of which dramatically improved services to patients; a young, aggressive CEO found out that her very aggressiveness was stifling the free flow of ideas and "collaboration" that she'd stated as a primary element in her business plan. In short, her staff was terrified of her. The success stories go on and on in financial services, global software applications, outsourcing, and in large and small government services.

This isn't because of a streak of luck but based upon an essential understanding of how the brain works, drawn from my years of training and practice as a neuropsychologist.

As children, we were constantly taught that we must have the right answer immediately lest we fail and be punished—a bad grade from a teacher or a scolding from a parent. The resulting behaviors are just the opposite of how we best function as adults. Critical thinking skills have never been more critical than now when we need to sort through mounds of information overload. The world may be flat in the mere exchange rate of information, but acquiring knowledge that is TRUE is no faster now than it was hundreds of years ago. Gaining wisdom is not a sprint sport.

As grown ups, when facing complex information systems in business, family interactions or emotional conflicts, we *can't* instantly come up with every answer every time. We need to allow ourselves to stand in the unknown for a little while, but what is more frightening than standing in the unknown, naked and without a solution? The first great challenge in my work is to get people to stop doing all the things they think they have to do to find the answers—and *not to tripwire* the "let me perform for you" instinct during high demand, high performance situations.

With the right *questions* and the skills taught to uncover half-truths, they can start to discover who they are, how they truly function, and how to use more of the resources that are uniquely available to them.

The second challenge is for me to realize that I'm a humble participant in this process, as I was back in the winter of 2000 with the student on the ledge. I'm an equal with the patient and the problems. The hierarchy of healing is no longer useful, because I'm not supposed to have all the right answers, either. That old reliable Us and Them mentality only slows us down.

Every successful business or businessperson needs a CRO, a Chief Reality Officer, which is where I step in. I'm not selling people or families or corporations a better future but rather the simple opportunity to discover what *can* come next. If they *just* do that (not a simple thing), the future moves toward them without interference. Put differently, what you *actually want to happen* ends up happening without you having to steer or control people and events.

The CEO of a Southern California firm said to me recently that he couldn't see the money value of doing this "soft stuff." He already had a company of people aligned with his ideas. I asked him if I could work with his managers for a while and gather their thoughts—for free. He agreed to this and was then shocked to learn that 65% of the biggest problems the managers dealt with were linked to questioning their core value alignment to the company's vision. He couldn't have known that because they'd consistently told their leader that they'd mastered the prototypical success tip and half-truth of "having a vision!"

I asked them to put an estimate on how much productivity was lost due to this single illusion. The consensus was that about half of the potential deals on the table would likely not come to fruition because of this one condition, at a total cost to the business of $750,000. The CEO had never realized this until now because his VPs were too busy convincing him that they had things "under control." Did he want his people to keep lying or did he want the $750,000?

After a year of coaching and consulting work with the Impact Group in St. Louis, I saw their growth in revenues increase by 46%. I did a turnaround at Davita, Inc, the country's largest dialysis company, boosting its employee retention rate nearly 20 percentage points for one of the harder retained clinic positions in one of its most challenging retention regions. As the CRO at both places, I worked with the key players in:

- Constantly linking individual actions to larger systems issues so people can see how being accountable isn't just a "boss's order" to control them but a way to create a shared goal

- Pushing comfort zones to say "the unspeakable" in meetings—naming the big pink elephant in the room

- Pointing out the presence of fear hidden behind a well-articulated solution

- Pulling out the under-the-radar-screen dialogue of employees that lie underneath their actual spoken words

- Constantly broadening a CEO's vision to include triple bottom line considerations (people, planet, profit)

Too many traditional models of coaching and healing start with how to get success—but even if it comes for a while, it isn't sustainable. You can't figure out How To until you know What Is. I teach *how we function* before I teach that we can achieve more success. If you understand that, you can sustain it forever.

My message has been getting around, especially in the world of business. I'm now working with executives representing such diverse organizations as Chevron, the Oriental Trading Company, Davita, Epsilon, the City of Calgary, and The Impact Group, just to name a few. Professional athletes, Juilliard musicians, and high-profile Hollywood executives have found their way into my office when trying to get beyond traditional models of change and high performance.

I've written for MSN.com and CFO.com, been cited as an expert by *The New York Times*, *Christian Science Monitor*, published articles for *Prevention Magazine* and other periodicals, while serving as an expert, regular columnist for the "Transformations" section of *Executive Decision*. And it's all because I've learned how to really help.

These cutting edge ideas aren't just appealing to innovative, start-up business but are also catching the eyes of more traditional firms. I've recently been asked to write a chapter in a book on hiring due out in 2008 and published by the premier training and development organization, The American Society of Training and Development.

From childhood through young adulthood and more intensely now as my practice expands, I've been shown the power of these ideas all around and within me. The exposure of half-truths allows for far more co-creation—instead of just co-existing with others. This applies to all the major areas of being human: our deepest interaction with ourselves, romantic relationships, work, business success, personal ethics, and what some might call magic, but there's no magic in it. There's just getting beyond the half-truths and using more of What Is.

THE GOD SHRINK &
THE SIX HALF-TRUTHS of
RELIGION

My dear friend Mike Novak and I met at the University of Notre Dame during graduate school as fellow musicians in the Folk Choir, an internationally known sacred music group. In 1997, we were bound for Ireland on a tour and little did I know that I would be transformed forever by his words in a smoky O'Hare Airport bar where we bonded over some port and had our first psychological/theological dialogue. I can remember that day as if it were yesterday, not just because of the things we talked about but because our friendship deepened to a level that would culminate with him standing by my side as my best man eight years later.

In many ways, the door to my understanding the half-truth logic in life started there, when he turned to me and said, "Kevin, you've got to read *The Screwtape Letters* by C.S. Lewis." As I tried to get more out of him about this book, he kept repeating himself, "Just read it." Ten years later, this book became my basis for uncovering and trying to overcome the many half-truths of our world.

In this classic novel, Lewis tells a story of an elder demon named Screwtape who, through his letters to a younger devil, shows how to subtly and elusively turn the human brain toward confusion—the best path on the gradual road to evil. Bring on doubt and clever rationalizations and you're on your way. Just as the devil doesn't walk up to your front door and say, "Hi, I'm evil, let me in," most of the other not-so-effective things in life and business don't come at you so clearly but hide behind, "Makes sense to me." It's in this spirit that my book was written—to help one sniff out all the "makes sense to me" things in business, psychology, and now in the murky realm of the Judeo-Christian religion. For those not religious or God-oriented per se, they can certainly read this section with a "spiritual" eye, as many of the half-truths are just as applicable for this mindset. It may even clear up confusions that have grown up around the whole religion-versus-spiritual "debate."

Half Truth #1: God is nonjudgmental.

In this half-truth we find our temporary peace in the knowledge that God is more compassion and mercy than judge and jury. Though this claim actually has strong theological tenets behind it, it's not so much its inaccuracy that poses a problem for us all but its application to our lives. But that's often the way half-truth logic works. It's not always in the claim itself, but in how we understand and apply it. How do we hear this statement about God and breathe its core wisdom into our bones and being? Do we reactively use it as a justification to put our wrong actions on the most peripheral aspects of our consciousness and call it ignorance? Do we bargain with God and use our ritualistic expressions of praise and worship as our timecard sheet into Heaven, while not being present spiritually with others but trying to ease our dissonance with this nonjudgmental God?

It is as if what is most dangerous here is not the statement itself (for it is true), but in the linking of events in a causal chain that can undo any divine and ultimate relationship we have with God in the first place. It's like taking pride in keeping a clean car as you drive it off a cliff to your death. What good is the comfort of a nonjudgmental deity when the life that, you hope, this nonjudgmental God "judges" non-judgmentally isn't well lived?

In my practice as a psychologist, I see that most of my patients are too worried about right and wrong and not worried enough about liv-ing **in general**. Jesus said, "I came to give you Life and *more of it*." Psychology has not helped this situation with decades of research and practice around soothing neurotic issues rather than healing them. As shrinks, we look for what's wrong more than we recommend "how to live." Ill practiced and poorly preached religion has added to this snow-ball by concentrating on sin, the bad nature of human beings, and what to do to avoid punishment versus living more closely with God.

This is not to say that there aren't objectively "evil" things out there that will remove you from the grace of God. And it's not to say that we shouldn't be aware of those things. But we need to know what to do when *not* doing those activities, which is where most of us live the great majority of the time. To me, that is far more critical and more defining of the oneness needed for salvation then reliance on a nonjudgmental God for the things we are not doing very well.

Half Truth #2: If you can feel God, He is present.

Seems obvious, doesn't it? The purest truth that this is TRYING to get to is this: WHEN you put your emotions in their proper place, you allow the fullness of God to be present in you. And, yes, that can give you a sort of fulfilling feeling. But I will bet all that I have that this is not what the Pentecostal and Fundamentalist religions are preaching when they attempt to link emotion and God together.

What we are not getting from the pulpit is good theology. Take bad theology and put that into a brain that craves stimulation and sensation, and you have a thunderstorm of misinterpretations and misguided efforts from otherwise well-intentioned people (and that is the BEST CASE scenario!). Take the other people whose hearts are misaligned and that will only make things worse.

There are two key points here:

1. Emotions come and go. There are really only a few major emotions, and the rest are learned and repackaged versions or combos of these. In other words, there is no such thing as feeling "bad." Bad is the result of other factors that produce that particular feeling. Emotions desire to self-perpetuate and live

on forever. Because they want to breed and multiply into mutated versions of truth or explanations of what we call truth, we think that God should have an accompanying emotion, and we also think that it should be a "good one." But some of the most magical moments "with God" are emotionless. And some of the most magical moments with God are with our deep PRIMARY emotions: Good and Bad (anger and joy). Given all this, how could emotions be so critically defining of the existence of God in one's life?

2. Theologically speaking, most faiths don't teach their congregations about "the dark night of the soul" when we feel that God is absent and has abandoned us. The lives of the saints are full of this notion in their mystical writings, and there is a consensus about how such an experience can open the doorway to wisdom. Is the absence of God ever actually real? If so, this brings up many questions about 1) Where exactly is our missing link, in sensory terms, to God and 2) Whether that, in and of itself, is a "weakness" of the individual's connection in the first place? To me, this perceived void is again one of those issues where being right, regarding its good or bad nature, doesn't matter. What matters is that, in terms of accessing and using the creative love all around us, this moment can lead to forgiveness of the past and a more aligned intention for action in the future. Much like the negative space that is necessary for a full appreciation in viewing a painting, we can't truly process a human life without some of this darkness.

Half-Truth #3: Love is primary.

"Love others as you love yourself."

We've all heard this many times, but if you're like me, you pondered one big hole in this statement when growing up and taking religion classes: What if you don't love yourself that much? Then how are you supposed to love others? Though no teacher ever disagreed with me on this point, I never really got a solid answer for dealing with those people who don't love themselves.

Are there a lot of these people? Are you one of them? Does that state of affairs in you negate any desire to love another in the first place? If not, then we have many people WANTING to love others but not knowing how and making, or repeating, terrible emotional mistakes. Here's where the exploration of this half-truth can help.

When you love yourself loving another person, that's narcissism. It is "loving yourself the world's way." The easy translation for this is selfishness. I think it's an understatement to say the world is changing fast and there is moral decay. At the center of all this decay is the self-centeredness of people. The emphasis now is on me, myself, and I. Many times people do things in a self-indulgent way, rationalizing its effect on other people, or do things regardless of what people think of them or what the outcome might be. That is not loving one's self in God's way. The difference between the casual phrase "loving yourself" and the truer meaning of "loving yourself" is the difference between being selfish and selfless when it comes to giving yourself to a relationship. And let me clarify: losing one's self in a co-dependent, identity diffusing, panicky sort of way is based more on fear than on love. What do I mean by this?

My clinical practice for years was filled with stories that would represent, in the half-truth metaphor consistent with this book, what I would call "half love." That is, the appearance of selfless love for another. Sounds really desirable, right? What could possibly make me think of this as half-love or well-intentioned intimacy? Most notably would be the indicator that these individuals were angry and resentful about their "loving behaviors." Didn't have to have a Ph.D. to see that one coming. To me, selfless love is love incarnate and certainly without rumblings within. Chances are if resentment is felt, it is not the highest of levels of love or even an aligned, healthier everyday "human" love. Like many half truths, we get our evidence from things that "make sense," and nothing can be more riddled with the sensory overload of this sometimes unfortunate state of affairs as this thing called love. In many of these therapy examples, a deep inadequacy about who one "is" at one's core is the driving factor towards a resentful enmeshing disguised as "giving it all to another."

If Love (capital L) is, in essence, God, the "half love" example above is most certainly not the selflessness that is of God because that motivation is unification and fullness for its own sake, not a merging of identities because *you* yourself are not good enough. Ironically, the giving to someone else in these cases is still all about one's self, not about giving.

In Ephesians 5:28-29a, the Bible says, "In the same way, husbands ought to love their wives as their own bodies. After all, no one hated his own body."

In the above verse, the Apostle Paul is assuming that men love themselves and the love he's talking about in his letter to the Ephesians is different from the love we know today. There are four Greek words for love (three are in the Bible and one is not): "Agape" = unconditional love; "Phileo" = conditional love' "Eros" = Sexual love; and "Storge" or "Astorgos" = love or lack of love, respectively, among family members. While the English Bible translated all three in the Bible with the word "love," each has its own meaning.

Loving others as you love yourself is not a simple concept or process. If you're anything like me, your teens and 20s (and, for some, 30s and later!) were full of messing this one up. How could it be so hard to practice this? My trap was that I was unaware my experience of love could be so much more. When I say more, I don't mean self-adoration but the "more" that is all-transforming for both people in the relationship. I was like a kid taking pride in his model car as the ultimate driving machine, not knowing there were real cars that were much bigger, faster, and, well, more real. As I matured and eventually found my true self inside my life partner, I could finally celebrate this type of love. So beware which meaning you want for the word "love" in the relationships you build with others—and with God.

Love may just be something you use merely to get by, as opposed to being what you truly want but don't yet know in its fullness. It is in this tension of forming the completeness of Love where many fall out of urgency to complete the circle—and end up writing a story of love for themselves that is not of God's standards. Despite all the zest and good intentions, this is still not really loving one's self.

Half Truth #4: Perfection is the utmost of goals desired by God from us.

Jesus mentioned that the Sabbath was made for man, not man for the Sabbath. What could this really mean? It has real significance for us in how we see what pleases God in this statement. Most of those in the pulpit implicitly teach the wrong perfection in getting closer to God. Are we meant to perfect our human behavior to the point of negating our humanity? Or can we be both human and close to God? Where is that point, that magical balance point?

What I see as a psychologist is a subtle yet dangerous trap that parallels obsessive-compulsive personality traits. If the core of this psychological disorder is to reduce the anxiety of things not "perfect" around or inside one's self, one seeks endlessly and with great fervor to minimize the dissonance of these imperfections. So what you get is an elaborate attempt at neutralizing what, in the eyes of God, might be a beautiful array of weirdness, oddities, and nuances that actually have meaning and importance that is, perhaps, unknown to us.

What I love personally about the Catholic faith is that celebration of uniqueness and culture. While fundamentalist faiths preach what they think is universal acceptance, they also teach subtle double binds to this idea ("Of course, we love you the way you are, but we'd love you more if you just ..."). This keeps the neuroticism of humanity alive and keeps humans thinking there are no solutions to these quandaries.

Case in point. I was recently asked by a client inquiring about the "craziness" of his family and what I thought the number one ingredient might be in a family system (and this might as well be a world system, too) that perpetuates dysfunction. Power? Abuse? Physical violence? All these things are negative, but I believe that introduction of the double bind is the greatest source of dysfunction, precisely because of the polarity problem that the helplessness creates, rendering creative love and action inept by fear. It focuses on dissonance reduction (not love creation) at all points in all relationships and keeps our wheels spinning, succeeding only at "the best way to stand still and go nowhere." We take pride in minor victories while losing the major battles for progress and finding optimal solutions.

God wants us, not our perfection. And in giving our hearts, we get a perfect relationship.

Loving a real person wholly is richer and more fulfilling than searching for a "love" based upon some notion of human perfection. Do we really believe this or do we merely occasionally and intellectually acknowledge it? Knowing the difference can be the difference between lasting joy and pleasurable moments.

Half Truth #5: Conflict is bad and is not of God.

If we believe that the ultimate virtue of God is harmony and being harmonious, than we are on another slippery slope. What if the harmony we are "causing" is precipitated by fear, avoidance, etc.? There are two types of sin: ones of commission and ones of omission. Could sins of omission lead us to a false sense of harmony?

The Old Testament is full of the God who serves vengeance up in a heartbeat, so we would seem to have good reason to take issue with the above half-truth. But on the other hand, we can't just take the stand that we should simply remind the pacifist whiners of the world about all the war-torn afflictions of the Old Testament, as if to say, "That is the language and those are the actions of God, so don't blame me for what's wrong now." We shouldn't try to justify the ills of today by pointing back toward the Bible.

Instead of resting on that reactive position, we are called to a co-creative place in which we can truly discern the criteria of spiritual justice behind what we choose as conflict and how we express it. This arises most notably in how and when we decide to fight wars.

The Catechism of the Catholic Church teaches, *"Anger is a desire for revenge."* Anger is a passion (emotion) by which a man reacts to evil, real or apparent, and seeks vindication of his rights; that is, justice. By itself, the passion is neither moral nor immoral but becomes so by reason of its being ordered or disordered—reasonable according to the circumstances. An ordered anger is directed at a legitimate object with an appropriate degree of vehemence. An inordinate anger is directed either at an illegitimate object or with an unreasonable vehemence. As

St. Thomas Aquinas notes, vice may be by defect as well as by excess. So the presence of evil *should* provoke a righteous anger which, if absent, constitutes a sinful insensibility."

What dovetails nicely here between my book's premise about the danger of half-truths and this age-old wisdom is that we are called to inquire and seek the fullness of a situation and to see whether war or heightening conflict is truly necessary. We are called to go to the "third response," beyond reaction and, then, beyond even the next reaction that is really a way to rationalize a more self-protected and comfortable notion—the notion that our actions are now truthful and just.

We must get beyond simple notions of good and bad to examine the nature of anger and its causes. I once had a very angry female patient who withheld sex from her husband because she was upset that he kept parking his old antique sports car in her garage spot, which obviously had nothing to do with sex or even broadly any intimacy concern. This is an example of the clever post-first-pause rationalizations we make. What was hers? After years of being walked over, she was setting a boundary, claiming that she was "using (my) teachings from therapy." It is not setting a healthy boundary when the motivation is not of a loving nature but of a vindictive intent.

Finally, God Himself creates things that are filled with conflict and pain. Consider that at about 10 p.m. on the night of May 4, 2007, a tornado hit Greensburg, Kansas, 110 miles west of Wichita. It was an F-5 twister, the so-called "Finger of God," and one of the biggest ever seen in America. A total of eight tornadoes touched down in southern Kansas that night and the National Weather Service reported dozens more. In Greensburg, ten people were killed, 95% of the town was destroyed, and the entire population had to be evacuated. The devastation resembled a huge hammer coming down on a village of 1,500 and wiping out a way of life. What do we make of this? The same thing we should make of the infinite beauty and complexity of God's other creations—which we pass every day going to work—without a moment's thought.

Half Truth #6: Spirituality and religion are two different things.

As C.S. Lewis wrote in *The Screwtape Letters*, the world is full of forces and people that pit two incomplete truths against each other when both are false and misleading. When one seeks to win with an incomplete truth, it makes him a temporary victor but a permanent loser. This is happening today with the concepts of "spirituality" and "religion." What we now hear about these areas are things like:

- I am not religious but more spiritual.

- Religion is the core of our world's problems. Without it, we wouldn't have all these fights.

- Going to church (being ritualistic with some religious expression) is better (with the implicit belief that something of "work and effort" is of more value than something without those things. That is, "it's the lazy people who call themselves more spiritual.")

What a mess. Each statement has wisdom in it, but it is as if the intentions or motivations underneath it undo any good. More dangerously, they have a self-fulfilling, insulated nature built into them. So, if you say this, then you can easily believe it and, in that belief, you feel justified in your stance. You're better than someone else who's touting one or the other point of view.

It's a very strange state of affairs that sets up a totally unnecessary and false dichotomy. You don't hear people say, "I've got too much money in my bank account" or "I've got too much good health." So why do this with religion and spirituality when both can be very useful in helping us live better lives?

In essence, the full natural life merges these two not because of some belief that one is more important then the other but because, when both are left to their own "devices" of being as they are, they naturally seek each other more. The spiritual person, if truly so, will naturally want to seek more outward expressions of piety and more celebrations of faith.

WHERE'S THE LIGHT IN ENLIGHTMENT? THE 7TH HALF TRUTH OF THE WORLD

Not long ago, I was sitting in a Good Friday Mass feeling run ragged by raising two babies and staring blankly at the cross. The self-justifying parts of me looked around and said, "What the hell are you doing here? You can't get anything out of Mass now … and, for that matter, let's forget Sunday Mass, as well, which has been a joke every week for over a year." I listened to this voice and, for a moment or two, it truly got to me. I realized that I hadn't really "heard" a reading in nearly two years. I'd lost any semblance of regularly praying in daily Mass and felt angry that even my "back up" morning liturgy of reading and studying my faith had been displaced by exhaustion and my two hours of sleep a night. I was falling into zombie-like behavior from the demands of parenting. In rare moments, I was fully lucid but was far more often distracted by feeding babies, cleaning up after them, and trying to eat and sleep. As I listened to the words, "Where you there when they crucified my Lord?" I felt angry and abandoned. When I closed my eyes and tried to pray, I thought about two things:

1) Either my Catholicism had failed me or I was in desperate need of some help and advice.

or

2) My anger/grief had nothing to do with loss of Catholicism but rather the loss of my self.

Then I realized how much of my faith before the days of being a father was riddled with self-indulgent comforts or at least the numbing distractions that had never really tested my own faith. I was in pain and decided to write to my friend, Mike Novak, now a doctoral theology student at Marquette University. What he wrote back was so moving and so pertinent to a discussion about enlightenment that I feel compelled to quote him at length:

"You've depended on the experience—and luxury—of attending daily Mass, and we've talked about how frustrating that loss was as your family grew and rightly demanded more attention from you. To a certain extent, these periods of luxury and ease of faith, where we have a liturgy by the Folk Choir at the University of Notre Dame, or a really gifted preacher who happens to preach in the ways or about the things that we get: these are like times of childhood for us, where we are allowed to feed, and learn, and concentrate on ourselves, even if we're not thinking so much about it in terms of self. Now you're in an 'output' time of your life. And the frustration is natural, and the weariness mounts. And you want the ease and sure, visible 'progress' of the 'input' times, because you could 'see' the 'spiritual' stuff you were doing. It's like teaching high school: nine months of output meant I HAD to have that 'input' time of summer break.

But that's the human side of it. On the divine side ... you can have those periods of the 'dark night,' as John of the Cross called it. God is absent. The void is increasingly real. And all of what seemed like the spiritual times, the content times, these now in retrospect look suspiciously like make-believe, and we doubt not only our faith now, but also our faith of the past. The prophets are full of complaints about this absence of God. Maybe reading the Psalms is what you want to be doing now: not so much for learning, for insight, but for commiseration. *Feeling* the same as the Psalmist.

And yet this is the time when Love will count the most. Like in athletics when the muscle grows only because you've moved past what you can do, and are now doing what you can't. The pain is ... real? Love is never compelled. And God overwhelming us with those times of spiritual comfort—that's great for us, that is, that FEELS great for us, but what really counts, what really teaches us to live, to become, *the love that God is*, is to move in love in those times where none of it makes sense or gives us satisfaction. When the feelings of contentment return, when the presence of God is obvious, that's when we look back and see that these times—and our faithful acts of love in them, even in diapers, lack of sleep, and a non-picture-perfect marriage. These times so increased our capacity for love of one another and of Christ. And the times of contentment look different to us as a result. It's in all the saints, all the journals everyone's ever written. All the wise know this, and you do, too. But right now it sucks. Move through it AS IF everything were still full of the feelings you're missing, and you'll find in the end that the void was a very small thing when you look back at it."

If that's wasn't enough to think about or work on, Mike then wrote a PS:

"The fact that the spiritual dryness would be 'doubled' with the time of your marriage having produced children is no surprise, because at the merely anthropological level you are *having* to be drawn out of yourself, and emptying yourself, in order to make marriage and fatherhood work, and to avoid being one of those failures who flees because he has to 'think of himself first.' As you rightly realize, *now* you are going to learn so much more about what love is—an act of the will, the fulfilled vow to *be* there—rather than just the good feelings. It's so easy to justify bailing out of our commitments today in terms of the psychobabble about good feelings and healthy self-identity, whereas the truth is that in doing so we only stunt our capacity to engage in that self-emptying love.

In theology, that's called *kenosis*: the 'self-emptying' that characterizes the love of Christ in the great Philippians hymn in Philippians 2: 5+: 'Christ emptied himself and became a slave....' It wasn't entirely that you weren't able to listen to the Passion accounts, although you could have certainly listened and profited more. You were *experiencing* some of that Passion, that self-emptying, and at a loss to make sense of it given your earlier easy, spiritual pleasure in God. You were *sharing* what Christ finally came to: not just the self-emptying of the choice of love (different than being 'drained' against your will: you have to freely *do* it) but that Jesus, too—The Logos made flesh, God Incarnate—came to share in that empty feeling, that lack of the experience of the presence of God, that we humans all share. Thus his quote of Psalm 22: 'My God, my God, why have you forsaken me?' This was his final, ultimate identification with us: to be lost in the silence of the absence of God, and yet still to make the God-choice: the trust, the faith, the affirmative of love. And thus he comes to the triumph of the resurrection, as we one day will who join into this choice of his as well...."

Enlightenment is actually not esoteric but very concrete and real, almost (paradoxically) as real as the most mundane moments of life. In this state, we find the ego truly absent. Whether one is a psychologist or a business consultant, this insight alone can color a whole set of recommendations on "self improvement" decisions for a lifetime's work. This is why the Enlightenment chapter truly is the 7th half-truth for everything else in this book.

As someone undertaking the mission of uncovering and rooting out half-truths, I felt it necessary to include here my own difficulties in this work. I'd hit a wall where I needed to re-conceptualize my understanding of my spiritual world as a man two years into a marriage with three kids, a blended family, an entrepreneurial venture, a book in progress, and all the pains and woes in between. Even as an author writing about the clever trap of self-absorption, I found myself slipping into it and sought counsel from a brilliant theologian who was the best man at my wedding. Mike's response to me was illuminating for this examination of how we THINK we've found enlightenment and why we shy away from and, inherently, devalue the ACTUAL criteria of true spiritual enlightenment. With Mike's help, I've undertaken a deeper exploration into this subject from a mostly Christian point of view.

As he puts it, and I agree, Christianity and Catholicism, in particular, are all about enlightenment and encourage the pursuit of this in all its forms. All truth is one, whether it's religious, scientific, artistic, interior or exterior. There are no contradictions in reality, even if we can't perceive that unity at any given moment. Yet, of course, there will still be disagreement on what constitutes enlightenment.

Christianity sees other religions, for example, as being valid paths to enlightenment … to a certain extent. The Spirit of God is perceived or sensed by all people, and human religion has been formed in response to that perception as understood from culture to culture. Yet Judaism and Christianity believe that God has acted publicly throughout history and that we are responsible to that initiative from God to understand Him as He hasrevealed Himself to us. In cases where the data of that revelation clashes with understandings of other religions, Christianity considers its insights to be of greater factual value in the face of such disagreement.

Problematically, "Enlightenment" has been turned into a commodity in our society—that the search for enlightenment has been reduced to a product that can be marketed and sold. An entire industry has grown up around it. But that, too, is part of the normal process of human communications, conversation, and debate.

At the same time, much of little quality and worth is produced, with many concepts of Enlightenment floating around that may not be so enlightened after all. A so-called "Enlightenment" that caters to mere feelings of self-worth or self-importance, that turns "Enlightenment" into merely a bauble or piece of self-decoration or self-glorification—a pleasure in the feeling of being enlightened—is not true enlightenment.

Judaism and Christianity are not centered on private revelations or teachings given to one prophet who then proclaims his insight to the rest of the world, not even from Moses or Jesus. The foundational events happened historically and publicly and are to be judged historically and publicly. Likewise, true enlightenment takes on a distinctly public character: love of God and love of our neighbor. The First Letter of John throws down the challenge, evoking the teaching of Jesus: "How can you say you love God, who you have never seen, when you don't love your brother, who you can see?"

Enlightenment is not about the self, but about relationship, and one of those relationships is with God. You can't be involved in *anything*—any event or perceived human difficulty—without its being a part of your creative connection to God. With that as a foundational understanding of What Is and of how you function, why do feel justified in blaming someone or something outside of you that's made you a victim? If you helped create whatever you're experiencing, then you have the power to change it. You have the choice to transform your experience—by going beyond talking about it to a therapist—into something other than a punishment of the self repeated countless times in a myriad of painful variations.

There's far more to life than coping or damping yourself down with lowering dissonance or swallowing pills. There's taking your own sense of self and your responsibility much deeper than you might have believed possible. You've helped make your past what it's been, so you can also help turn it into the future you want.

Power starts with this realization of your connection to and interaction with more than you can see or consciously know (call it the unconscious or God—the very thing we were never allowed to talk about or acknowledge in grad school in psychology; my teachers were terrified of letting God into the conversation). This one idea of interacting with the unseen expands the psychological paradigm by which I felt limited ever since starting my study of this discipline and working my way toward a Ph.D. It combines the necessary training of the head, which my field is good at, with the bottomless wisdom of the heart in ways that make one plus one equal far more than two.

Such enlightenment changes the self yet can require incredible attention to the self, depending on the shape it takes, and the history of Christian spirituality shows us that it comes in forms as varied as those of all humanity and human activity itself. But enlightenment is never merely ABOUT the self. There is only one thing or state that is solely about the absorption of self in and about the self in Christian thought, and we call that Hell.

True enlightenment sees that the self is utterly related to Creator and creation, in God and all others, and lives itself out that way. Any so-called enlightenment that doesn't come near to this fact is unworthy of the name.

EPILOGUE

Orange County—with all the money and superficiality one associates with this part of the country. I should have been leery or at least cautious about accepting the version of reality they serve up in Southern California when the airline pilots tell you that the planes flying into and out of Orange Country Airport have to shut off their engines for a moment while flying over certain neighborhoods due to noise ordinances. On this brisk and beautiful April day, when I arrived for my first day of consulting with a new premier and high profile executive development retreat program, that should have raised my ability to be skeptical about what was coming. I was already dealing with people on the fringe.

I'd signed a contract with a facility in one of the wealthiest beach communities in the world and was offering a unique blend of executive coaching to the "derailed executive with addictions." I was being flown in each week from my home in Jackson Hole to provide a combination of executive and organizational effectiveness training with my years of clinical practice in treating those with addictions. My goal? To work with the crème de la crème of wealth, power, influence—and, yes, narcissism—and invite these businessmen, NFL players, rock star musicians into a different world of "therapy." This one wouldn't have them sitting on a couch with a Freudian know-it-all spewing family background hypotheses about why they were in trouble. That wouldn't work here. Their backgrounds had, in some ways, served them well. They were more successful and more powerful than I was and had far too many reasons to consider me, the treatment provider, to be the one who needed their advice.

So I had my work cut out for me. The owner of this facility saw a niche for me and had read one of my magazine articles. She knew these people 1) were addicts, 2) had too many counter reasons not to listen to most anyone out there trying to help them, 3) could manipulate on a level above and beyond the already high level that is characteristic of addiction populations generally and, yet, 4) needed a connection point, an engagement point into a new way of looking at their situation. So she called me.

How was I going to do this, a 34-year-old with degrees but no real way to show "my stripes" to these people nor a Swiss bank account that proved my influence and wealth?

I began by thinking: What if they were NOT the odd ones who needed a magical person with the right resume and a perfect Renaissance background to be the Christ-figure and heal them? What if they were just like me and so many others but had gone to florid and disturbing extremes that I'd never seen or ventured to explore? What if we are all addicted to being someone we weren't, to spinning stories, to living lies and half-truths, to building false egos, to hurting people (but with good intentions), to looking like and being an "as if" so much so that we actually think we *are* real? What if these extremely addicted folks around us are here to make us feel better about our own crippling but not so visible addictions? They are the ones wearing the red bullseye on their chests, the most visceral and tangible examples we have of what convinces us we are not. So they just "need our prayers."

Yeah, right.

Maybe this calls for two guitars, a ledge, and a bridge yet again between the Us and the Them.

As I rode in their limo from the airport to the facility, I reminded myself of this grounded logic, which was lodged deep in my heart. And as I looked out at the sunset over the Pacific Ocean, I felt at peace; a peace that overrode my sense of fear and intimidation. It's funny how, sometimes, one needs the most potentially intimidating of all scenarios to push one to that point of either falling apart or—at last—being willing to get real. Without these moments, we might all choose to be pleasantly numb and antiseptic in our own lives, immune to the necessary shake-ups that are all choice points of standing up or sitting down. Thinking such thoughts and welcoming this opportunity, I broke into a half-smile as we pulled into the driveway of this beautiful home overlooking the water.

"Certainly no lack of stimulation for these people," I joked with the chauffeur as he got out and assisted me with my bags. "I thought the idea was to get them to detox off of highs." We laughed and then I guess he felt a need to make sure I wasn't feeling too carefree about this job.

"Now you know you are 'on' the moment you walk in there, right?" he said.

"Absolutely," I said, but inside I was experiencing a moment of doubt. I wouldn't even get to shower and freshen up or put my notes in order. Nothing. Just lights, camera, and full action. As I look back, this was probably the best thing for me. If given more time, I would probably have used it to build up safe and protective walls in order to "sound good" versus "being real and effective." But no guru could have convinced me of that wisdom as I walked up the long winding walkway to the door where I was greeted by an assistant.

"Welcome, Dr. Fleming. Flight good?"

"Oh, yes, wonderful. Loved hearing that your planes like to glide into the airport. Brings a warm fuzzy in me."

"Yeah, kind of odd, isn't it?" he said.

Then he mentioned that the group of seven people were anxiously awaiting me, the "new guy" on staff. In the language of addiction, "anxiously awaiting" translates into "can't wait to tell this new guy how much he doesn't know."

Using a most impressive and serious tone of voice, the assistant ran down the roster and said, "Doc, you have a real eclectic mix here. You have a former CEO of a multibillion dollar global operation, a former NFL player, an opera singer, a prominent lawyer from the Pacific Northwest, a billionaire who just flew in and is de-toxing but may be out to join the group later, as well a gay man who is the son of one of the wealthiest men in Monaco."

If my inner dialogue in the limo wasn't enough to get me derailed, hearing this certainly was. But again, something inside remained peaceful. Why? With an arsenal of this kind of talent, money, and ego awaiting me in the next room, I could forget about being wittier or craftier than they were. That wasn't going to happen. Something else had to be happening … and then it hit me. The only thing that could put me on their level was the truth. I wasn't richer or smarter and didn't have any magic up my sleeve. Just be the truth, I told myself as I entered the room. Just say it and have no fear.

My confidence was instantly shattered by a six-foot-eight-inch man looming over me. It had to be the ex-NFL player for, if this was an opera singer, I hadn't seen one like him on PBS. He wouldn't fit on stage.

As I reached out my hand to shake his, he said, "Who the fuck are you and what is your drug?"

I know many greetings in this world and have experienced quite a few, but this one was unique. Talk about getting right to my need to be the truth. Why doesn't God allow you to warm up a bit first? I had some nice Notre Dame football stories for this guy, but that wasn't how we began.

As I was about to answer, I noticed that all the others who'd been milling around the room stopped and grabbed a seat, waiting for me to speak or crumble right in front of them.

"I don't have a drug like yours, or yours, or yours," I said, pointing at him and then at the others. "But I'm an addict like you. And it's probably more painful for me because there is no twelve-step group that listens to my bullshit about how I'm normal and just fine."

Total silence.

Then more silence.

If I was about to be escorted back to the limo, I was ready to go. Instead, the NFL player shook my hand, spoke his name, and walked me over to the group.

As I told them about the invisible drugs and half-truths of this world, the ones that I and so many others were susceptible to, I also gave them a mission—to help the rest of us discern and work on our own intoxications and addictions.

In the coming months, I offered them a role they'd never had and very different from those offered by their past cognitive behavioral therapists. It was a partnership that was more than just a trite "Let's pretend we're equals." They were to assume a truly "equal" status with me and together we would learn that their substance of choice was not really a drug or alcohol but their way of abusing themselves through the use of half-truths.

Somewhere during our time together, each of these people had turned to a substance to support some half-truth that probably got them thinking they could skirt the laws of accountability in nature for a bit, while yearning to be both of this world and not in it.

And how were they different from me? Not very. When that became our starting point, they were willing to open up and work with me, and much was accomplished.

As I write the closing lines of the book, I must remember not to hold on too tightly to the words on the prior pages. In other words, like everyone else, I have to remember to be open and humble. Half-truths are always operating, multiplying, mutating, and splitting off, creating newly disguised ones every nanosecond of life and attempting to outwit the next enlightened individual who thinks he or she has figured it all out. As soon as we get comfortable with one "What is," it changes into something else.

So take these words and use them to begin the process of being more aware and more alive. Go forward with accountability, love, and without the fear of being authentic and true. Don't settle for half a life when a full one is just waiting for you to show up and live it. Don't settle for a half-asked life.

ACKNOWLEDGMENTS

I would like to thank first and foremost my incredibly kind wife Fran who gave me the courage to start writing down the thoughts that make up this book. Whether it was her unwillingness to have another dinner conversation transformed over into some "deep thought dialogue" or not, I don't care; I'm grateful for her seeing in me what I didn't see for so long: a voice to help change the world. Thank you, babe. I love you.

Tom Morris, whose kindness is simply unparalleled. Thank you for giving me a chance. From the first day we walked the beaches together in Wilmington, I knew I'd found a deep friendship and mentoring that would bring me both happiness and success. Your belief in me will never be forgotten.

Mike Taylor, whose patience and mentorship brought out the businessman in me and assisted me in leaving behind the righteous rationalizations of the academic. Your insights and wisdom make an exciting prospect for me as we grow our partnership together.

George Howard, who first taught me the benefits of challenging psychological thought. You gave me my "first shot in the big leagues" of higher education and presented me an opportunity to get a Ph.D. when my GRE scores told most institutions not to. Thank you for allowing me to start my psychological career by welcoming my questioning nature, my skepticism, and my distinctively alternative thinking. It predisposed me to find my identity on the tail ends of the bell curve!

Mike Novak, whose friendship over the years has been an irreplaceable resource for my mind and spirit. Your wisdom as my "wing man of theology" will be something I treasure for the rest of my life. It was you who brought me to C.S. Lewis, and your knowledge of mystical authors blew off the doors of my traditional library. Most of all, I thank you for walking next to me during the darkest periods of my life and helping me shine the light on those times and bring out the truth.

Gaetano Vaccaro and our random encounter at Moonview Sanctuary. Thank you for your brilliant comment about my fear of stepping out and taking my message forward. I never knew this until you nailed me on it that day. The special quality of our encounters is based not upon how frequently we meet but the depth of your words when we do.

Paul, Sophia and Maximilian who still loved their dad while he was buried in a basement late at night writing this book. Your unconditional love for your father is not taken for granted.

Steve Singular, whose writing eye, kind soul, and passion for helping me find my voice is second to none. While many have opened doors for me through their gestures of kindness, you literally carved insights out of me and put them on to paper. My brain did not like this exercise and had to die many times before rejoicing in this product.

Phillip Wren, who offered me a regular columnist position with his magazine, *Executive Decision*, when he had no reason to—I was just a no name with a vision on the transformation of business thinking.

David Weeks and Patch Adams, pioneers of eccentric thinking and research. Your connections and spirit live in these pages and I'm grateful for having found you in our dialogues together. I have the utmost respect for you.

Laura Herring, who gave my mind a shot as a new guy on the block in the executive coaching world. I'll never forget your belief in me. Thank you.

For all my friends, colleagues, clients, and supporters who've been there for me with uplifting emails, phone calls, and letters telling me to not give up.

Last but not least, to my Mom and Dad, because you gave me life and love. Thank you for making a place in your hearts for this eccentric, quirky fellow to feel at home.

978-0-595-45708-3
0-595-45708-8